A Handbook of Content Literacy Strategies

75 Practical Reading and Writing Ideas

A Handbook of Content Literacy Strategies

75 Practical Reading and Writing Ideas

Elaine C. Stephens

Jean E. Brown

Christopher-Gordon Publishers, Inc.
Norwood, Massachusetts

Credits

Every effort has been made to contact copyright holders for permission to reproduce borrowed material where necessary. We apologize for any oversights and would be happy to rectify them in future printings.

Interviews for Author's Perspective were conducted by permission of: Joan Bauer, Janet Bode, Eve Bunting, Russell Freedman, Joyce Hansen, Will Hobbs, Jim Murphy, and Dorothy Hinshaw Patent.

Christopher-Gordon Publishers, Inc.
1502 Providence Highway, Suite 12
Norwood, MA 02062
(800) 934-8322

Printed in the United States of America
10 9 8 7 6 5   06 05 04 03

Library of Congress Catalogue Number: 99-74262
ISBN: 0-926842-96-X

Acknowledgment

Collectively we have taught more than 50 years in public schools, colleges, and universities. We have worked with many creative students, dedicated teachers, and fine administrators. This book reflects their profound influence on us, and our desire to give something tangible back to them.

Several individuals have given us specific assistance and support with this project. Our heartfelt appreciation is extended to the following notable authors of young adult and children's literature who contributed their perspectives: Joan Bauer, Janet Bode, Eve Bunting, Russell Freedman, Joyce Hansen, Will Hobbs, Jim Murphy, and Dorothy Hinshaw Patent. Our appreciation also goes to Jon Zdrojewski, math teacher, Cass City, Michigan; Robert V. Anderson, Social Studies Coordinator for the Midland Public Schools, Midland, Michigan; Dee Storey, Professor of Teacher Education and Chair of the Middle School, Secondary, and Reading Department at Saginaw Valley State University, Michigan; and Nadine Burke, Professor of English, Delta College, Michigan. Finally, the graduate students in TE 520 and TE 615, fall semester, 1998, Saginaw Valley State University gave us valuable feedback on the title of this book.

We thank our editor, Sue Canavan, production manager, Laurie Maker, and formatter, Lynne Schueler, for their skillful and professional work with the manuscript. We also thank the reviewers for their perceptive insights and helpful suggestions: Gerald J. Calais, Associate Professor, McNeese State University, LA; Michelle A. Johnston, Executive Director, Northern Lower Michigan Leadership, Teaching, and Learning Consortium; Deborah Ann Sulzer, Senior Administrator for Instruction, Orange County Public Schools, Orlando, FL.

And most important of all, we are grateful to our family members who make it all worthwhile: Opal, Wes, Melinda, Tom, Griffin, Mitchell, Iza, Mary, Vesta, Diane, and Frank.

Dedication

For my lovely new grandaughter, Iza Marie Graham.
—ECS

In memory of my first teacher, my mother, Iza Maria Richardson Brown.
—JEB

Contents

Strategies by Chapter

CHAPTER 6

Alphabetical List of Strategies

Author Perspectives

INTRODUCTION

We have written *A Handbook of Content Literacy Strategies* to provide elementary, middle school, and secondary teachers with strategies for integrating reading and writing as tools for learning in the content areas. It is designed to help teachers develop instructional practices that enable students to become more active learners of content. This book demonstrates the partnership between reading and writing and responds to the standards movement by providing teachers with strategies to bridge these mandates with the realities of their implementation in today's classrooms. We describe content literacy strategies that have the power to make standards come alive for students and include procedures, classroom variations, and examples for each strategy.

With an ever-increasing knowledge base for each content area, students need to learn ways in which they can make the necessary connections among concepts, ideas, and even broad subject areas. Strategies for content literacy provide them with the means to make these types of connections.

While this book is intended primarily for teachers to use in their classrooms and with professional development, it is also appropriate for use in various graduate and pre-service education courses. Experienced teachers, beginning teachers, and pre-service teachers in elementary, middle, and secondary schools will find sound theory translated into practical classroom applications. For example, this book can be used in general methods courses, as well as for methods in specific content areas courses, and also in courses in reading and writing in the content areas. It can serve as a resource for teachers, a handbook for professional development, and a complement to content reading and writing textbooks.

A special feature of this book is the incorporation of literature, both fiction and nonfiction, to help students connect, explore, and expand their understanding of content knowledge. We believe that literature provides students with opportunities to connect ideas with realistic or even futuristic situations and experience them vicariously. Throughout the book we feature highly respected authors of young adult and children's literature. The feature, An Author's Perspective, consists of biographical information, the author's personal reflections, and a list of selected titles. We also include a specific chapter with strategies for using literature in all classrooms and recommended books and authors. The appendices provide additional information about award-winning books and sources for locating titles appropriate for various content areas.

A second special feature of this book is the emphasis on technology throughout the chapters. We provide classroom applications for the Internet, e-mail, and CD-ROMs.

In Chapter 1, we establish the need for and purpose of content literacy. In Chapter 2, we provide a theoretical framework for content literacy instruction. In Chapters 3, 4, and 5, we operationalize each component of the instructional framework. We present strategies in these chapters using the following format:

Strategy: (name of the content literacy strategy)

Component: (shaded box with bold text designates the primary component from the instructional framework: initiating, constructing, utilizing)

Content Literacy Process: (shaded box with bold text designates the primary language processes used in the strategy: reading, writing, speaking, listening, viewing)

Organizing for Instruction: (shaded box with bold text designates the primary grouping patterns: individual, pairs, small group, whole class)

Description: (concise overview of the strategy)

Procedures: (step-by-step directions for using the strategy)

Variations: (modifications that make a strategy applicable in a wide number of situations and content areas)

Examples: (brief descriptions of classroom use or sample formats for the strategy).

We use a slightly different approach in Chapter 6, providing teachers with information about appropriate literature for various content areas, how to locate it, and strategies for involving students with it.

CHAPTER 1

Content Literacy: Identifying the Issues

♦ ♦ ♦

On September 9, Superintendent Blair spoke to the district-wide School Improvement Committee. He began by saying, "Good afternoon. This committee is charged with creating a K-12 plan to address the continued poor performance of our students on state and national tests. Too many students score at unacceptable levels on assessments of reading and writing. We have a serious public relations problem and simply can't ignore the high stakes impact of testing. Your mandate is to implement content standards and improve assessment results."

Kevin Barkley, in his fourth year of teaching middle school science, began the discussion: "My students have a terrible time with writing. Last year I tried to have them write more in connection with the new core curriculum in science. But it was a major ordeal for many of them just to write a complete sentence, let alone anything more substantial. As for being able to read the textbook, forget it!"

Louise Garcia, a fifth grade teacher, agreed. "I have that problem, too, plus my kids think reading the social studies book is dull and boring. How do I help them use reading and writing in social studies and at the same time get them excited about it and see connections with their own lives? And oh, by the way, also find a way to implement content standards and prepare for the state assessment tests?"

Bryan Jefferson, with twenty years experience teaching high school math, responded. "We're being asked to do more and more and I wonder when I'm going to have time to do it all. One of my frustrations is that my students view math as a series of numerical calculations with right and wrong answers rather than as a problem-solving process."

♦ ♦ ♦

The teachers in this scenario, like many other teachers, are concerned and frustrated, but also seeking new ways to help their students become more successful learners. In this chapter, we address several questions that teachers frequently ask about how content literacy can help to meet their students' needs.

What is content literacy?

Is content literacy only reading and writing?

Why teach reading and writing after elementary school?

Why aren't textbooks enough for content teaching?

How do I integrate content literacy strategies into my curriculum?

We also include An Author's Perspective featuring award-winning author Russell Freedman.

What is Content Literacy?

Content literacy is most often defined as using reading and writing as tools for learning subject matter. Teachers who make content literacy a priority understand how students learn. Their goal is to help students learn content while developing the literacy and thinking skills necessary to become independent, lifelong learners. Content literacy is based upon constructivist theories which explain learning as a meaning-making process (Graves & Graves, 1994). Providing students with multiple opportunities to construct meaning in subject matter classes enhances their content knowledge and promotes a deeper conceptual understanding of it.

Content knowledge is to content literacy as an automobile is to an engine. While the knowledge of subject matter is the framework, it needs something to propel it. Content literacy strategies are vehicles to transport students beyond rote learning to higher-order thinking. To expand on the automobile/engine analogy, content learning is the journey with lifelong learning as the destination. There is a cumulative advantage to this type of learning—the more students know about a subject, the easier it is for them to acquire new knowledge. This, in turn, generally increases their receptivity to engaging in additional learning experiences.

Content literacy strategies engage students in actively reading textbooks and other related print materials; these strategies assist students in using writing to construct meaning, reflect upon it, and apply it. Irvin et al. (1995) describe strategies as ". . . processes that help students become thoughtful and deliberate in their approach to a specific learning task such as reading or writing. A student who can efficiently solve the problem demanded by such a task is said to be 'strategic'" (p. 4). Strategic learners are actively engaged in using content literacy strategies to process information, construct knowledge, and make critical judgments.

But in too many classrooms, it is the teacher who is actively engaged while students assume a passive stance toward learning. Vacca and Vacca (1996) remind us that, "Learning with texts is an active process. Yet assigning and telling are still common teaching practices and often have the unfortunate consequence of dampening students' active involvement in learning" (p. 23). When teachers recognize the importance of content literacy, they teach students to use content literacy strategies. Using these strategies increases students' abilities to internalize content knowledge and to develop conceptual understanding of subject matter.

In the following scenarios, we see how two teachers make learning positive and interactive in their classrooms.

Mitchell Ortez, a middle school math teacher, has observed his students' attitudes improve and their test scores increase since he started using journals and a variety of supplemental reading materials such as newspapers, advertising flyers, math riddles, and brain teasers. In their journals, students explain how they solve these problems and then create their own "real life" word problems demonstrating the math processes they are learning.

Sara Frabotta found her previously reluctant social studies students clamoring for more after she organized them into teams to research issues using the Internet and primary sources. Their work culminated in a magazine that they published and distributed throughout the school and community.

Mitchell and Sara and many other teachers have found that promoting content literacy by implementing content literacy strategies has a powerful impact on student learning and thinking. Throughout this book, we will focus on the interrelationships among reading, writing, and thinking to foster not only content learning, but also lifelong learning.

Is Content Literacy only Reading and Writing?

While our primary focus in this book is on improving student content literacy through developing their strategic use of reading and writing, it is important to place content literacy within the broader context of how all the language processes foster learning (see Figure 1.1).

Vacca and Vacca (1996) equate content literacy with using language to learn. Moore et al. (1998) quote Neil Postman (1979) to confirm that the study of content areas is really the study of language:

> Biology is not plants and animals. It is language about plants and animals. History is not events. It is language describing and interpreting events. Astronomy is not planets and stars. It is a way of talking about planets and stars. (p. 165)

Listening, speaking, and viewing contribute significantly to learning subject matter. Content literacy is an important part of performance-based classes such as music, art, drama, and physical education. Students in these areas use language for

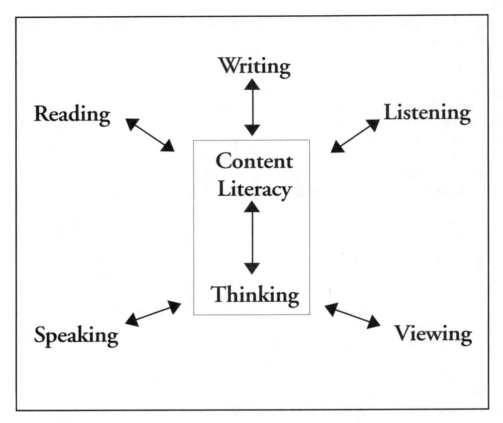

Figure 1.1

learning, too, and can benefit from content learning strategies. While reading and writing may not have as major an emphasis in these classes as in other content areas, teachers in performance-based classes have a unique opportunity to influence their students' attitudes toward reading and writing. They are in a favorable position to demonstrate to students their personal uses of reading and writing in their disciplines and their real-life application.

In many situations, students are expected to learn by listening for a significant portion of class time. Rarely, however, are they taught *how* to learn through listening, including responding strategies and notetaking skills. Helping students to listen effectively makes them better learners and more effective communicators. Creating opportunities for purposeful student talk between learning partners, in small groups, or with the whole class helps students to clarify their understanding and views as they combine new knowledge with prior knowledge. Experiences that give students multiple opportunities to use all of their language processes to interact with and internalize new concepts, ideas, and information increase interest and improve learning. In this book we also will describe listening and speaking strategies that help student increase their content learning.

Why Teach Reading and Writing after Elementary School?

Traditionally, misconceptions about how students learn to read and write have influenced instruction in content classes. Many educators used to believe that basic reading instruction was predominately the responsibility of early elementary teachers; upper elementary teachers would later teach more advanced reading skills. For the most part, reading was considered to be "learned" by the time children finished elementary school. Teachers thought that students learned to read in the elementary grades, and thereafter automatically used their reading abilities to learn from textbooks in various subject areas. But as Manzo and Manzo (1997) remind us, not all students are proficient in reading by the end of elementary school; and in middle school and high school even those who are proficient encounter increasingly complex and technical material that requires more sophisticated (and often different) reading abilities and higher-level thinking.

Concurrently, although many teachers used to believe that learning to write was more complicated and required more years of instruction than reading, it was considered to be almost exclusively the responsibility of language arts or English teachers. Again, teachers thought that once students had developed certain writing skills, they could automatically apply them in all subject areas. When students had trouble reading content textbooks or completing writing assignments, it was assumed that other teachers had not done their jobs or that the students were either unmotivated or slow learners.

Teachers and students often have other misconceptions that further complicate their understanding of reading and writing as processes for learning subject matter. A common assumption is that once students learn to read, they can read almost anything. It must be recognized, however, that not all reading tasks are the same. In other words, we frequently ignore the different thinking demands required for reading narrative and expository texts. For example, reading a short story requires different thinking processes than reading a chapter in a chemistry textbook. Interpretation differs from analysis and application. Moss, et al. (1997) recognize this problem: "Thus, in American classrooms, narrative literacy continues to eclipse information literacy at precisely the time when the ability to read and write exposition is, arguably, becoming more critical in our society" (p. 419).

A parallel situation exists in writing instruction. A common pattern is to provide elementary students with writing experiences based heavily on retelling personal narratives and creating stories. While teachers work hard to develop writing skills and encourage creative thinking, a serious problem arises when narrative is the only writing mode used in most classrooms. As Moss, et al. (1997) recognize ". . . if children are to become truly literate, they need opportunities to read and *write* in response to expository texts. . . . Teachers persist in the perennial *story* writing assignment, rather than affording children opportunities to explore other forms" (p. 419). A dramatic shift occurs for many students, however, when they enter middle school or high school. Frequently, it is assumed that students can write analytical responses to reading informational texts. The differences between writing stories and using expository modes to inform, describe, persuade, explain, or critique too often remain untaught.

Each of the following scenarios describes teacher frustration.

Lisa Ramey is frustrated. She carefully planned exciting earth science lessons using lots of visual aids and hands-on activities, but when she asked her class to read the textbook, it was a disaster. Her students seem smart enough, so what is the problem?

Ryan Cole tried giving an essay test to his history class because he wanted his students to write more, but the scores were so low that he felt over-whelmed and discouraged. "I'm not an English teacher," he thought. "I don't know how to teach them to write."

Michelle Nichols uses writing workshop and literature circles with her language arts class and is excited by how well they respond and how much they learn. "I've really been able to accommodate their varying needs and abilities, but I dread teaching the other subjects," she confided to a friend. "Something is missing. I've fallen into a deadly routine of assigning them to read a chapter and then answer the questions at the end of it. Sometimes we read the chapter aloud in class and discuss it, because I know many of my students can't read the material on their own. They're bored; I'm bored; but I don't know what else to do."

These teachers are hard-working, caring teachers who want their students to learn, but they have some mistaken assumptions about how students use reading and writing as tools for learning subject matter. Our understanding of how students learn has changed and developed extensively in the past few decades. We have more knowledge about the processes of reading and writing and thinking and how they are interrelated. We now understand that while the basics of reading can be learned in a few years, the application of reading as a tool to learn subject matter doesn't occur automatically and is most effectively learned when taught within the context of specific content classes. Equally important is our understanding that writing can be a powerful tool for learning subject matter if students are provided with appro-priate instruction.

Why aren't Textbooks Enough for Content Teaching?

The school curriculum is frequently textbook-driven. Teachers often make decisions about what to teach based upon the content of an adopted subject matter text. There are many reasons for this dependence on textbooks: teachers may feel more comfortable when using a familiar tool; or there is the practicality of using what is available; or there is the economic reality that schools expend the majority of their instructional budgets on expensive textbooks; or there is the misconception that subject matter knowledge is delivered best in textbook format. Regardless, the use of textbooks is extremely limiting in an information age when content knowledge is constantly increasing. Palmer and Stewart (1997) support this notion: "The stage is set for content area instruction in which extended, meaningful reading from a variety of books plays a central role and the dominance of a single textbook accompanied by teacher lecture is reduced" (p. 631). The inclusion of other sources of materials encourages student interest and involvement.

Teachers who make a serious commitment to incorporating content literacy into their classes find a wide range of varied media invaluable. The current explosion in technology offers a rich array of exciting opportunities for interaction and meaningful learning in virtually every subject area. Few people ever develop a passion for science or history or any other subject by reading a textbook. But a lively account of the origin of the solar system or a biographical account of Emma Edmonds masquerading as a man so that she could spy for the Union Army during the Civil War can fuel the imagination of youthful learners and inspire them to seek even more information. Print and multimedia materials are available about young people involved in efforts to clean up the environment or young people with special talents in music, art, or athletics or young people working with the elderly or the homeless or members of other groups in need. Math and science teachers can make connections between their course content and science fiction. Accurate and colorful historical fiction puts a human face on those times and events that students read about in their history texts. Well-conceptualized and well-written trade books, CD-ROMs, primary documents, and Internet resources provide students with reading and writing experiences that reflect the world beyond the classroom. The following scenario describes one teacher's approach.

Ann Wong has a group of reluctant students in her general science class. She keeps a number of scientific magazines and journals in her classroom as well as extensive files of newspaper clippings which students can read. Students also have access to a wide array of resources via the classroom computer. Ann found the students' enthusiasm increasing when she adapted a strategy entitled, Do you know . . .? (see Chapter 6) so that students present a connection between one of the scientific concepts they were learning in class and something occurring in the "real world."

◆ ◆ ◆

An Author's Perspective
RUSSELL FREEDMAN

Russell Freedman grew up in San Francisco and served in the Korean War. Early in his career, he worked as a reporter and editor for The Associated Press and then as a publicist for several network television shows. He now lives in New York City where he is a full-time writer. He is the author of more than 40 books, many of them award-winning, on a wide variety of subjects from animal behavior to history, including biographies. Among the awards his books have received are the Newbery Medal, Orbis Pictus, Washington Post Children's Book Guild Nonfiction, and ALA Best Book for Young Adults. Mr. Freedman was honored with the Regina Medal in 1996 and the Laura Ingalls Wilder Medal in 1998 for his body of work.

I try to write books that people will want to read willingly and with pleasure. I want students to read my books because they are interested in the subject, not because they have to write school assignments. Young people are a great audience to write for because they're so receptive and so appreciative. No author could have a better audience. The books you write for those readers may be with them for the rest of their lives. Often your book might be the first they have ever read on that particular subject. They will come to it with an open mind and with great expectations.

You're writing for a highly impressionable audience. They may never again read that much and they may never again be so profoundly affected. You have a readership that really wants to be told something, that wants to learn. It is a heavy responsibility, but it is also an exhilarating challenge.

I can't remember a time when I didn't want to write. My first book was the result of an article I read in the *New York Times* about a sixteen-year-old blind boy who had invented a Braille typewriter. That article aroused my curiosity, curiosity led to research, and research revealed that a surprising number of young people had earned a place in history before they were twenty years old, including Louie Braille, who also was blind and sixteen when he perfected the system of Braille. That gave me the idea for my first book, which was *Teenagers Who Made History.*

I feel very fortunate that I have been able to spend my working life writing books on subjects that interest me. I want to convey my enthusiasm for these subjects to the reader and I want to convey my point of view. Good nonfiction writing has to be factually accurate, but it never can be totally objective. There is no such thing as total objectivity. I believe that an author's personal vision of the material should come through in a nonfiction book. And I think of myself as a storyteller, not in the sense of inventing scenes or imaginary people and events, but in the sense of using storytelling techniques to ignite the reader's imagination. It is important to dramatize factual accounts of history; it's important for readers to picture people and events and to hear those people talking.

Since I write nonfiction, my books require quite a bit of research. For my Lincoln biography, I followed the Lincoln trail from his log cabin birthplace in Kentucky to Ford's Theater in Washington, D.C. and the rooming house across the street where the President died. There is something magical about being able to lay your eyes on the real thing, something you can't get from reading alone. When I wrote about Lincoln, I could picture the scenes in my mind's eye. Some of my research is devoted to finding archival photographs. It is a real thrill! There is something about seeing an old photograph that evokes a sense of history in a way that nothing else can.

Starting a new book is a lot like trying to solve a puzzle. You have to decide what to include and what to leave out, what to emphasize, where and how to balance facts and interpretations, and how to breathe life into the subject.

People spend so much time with television, which tends to perpetuate stereotypes. A stereotype is alienating—it makes it even more difficult to understand the experiences of others. A good nonfiction book should help to dispel stereotypes and make it easier for the reader to understand the experiences of others.

(Source: Interview with Russell Freedman, 1993)

Selected Titles

Buffalo Hunt	*Kids at Work: Lewis Hine and the Crusade Against Child Labor*
Children of the Wild West	
Cowboys of the Wild West	*The Life and Death of Crazy Horse*
Dinosaurs and Their Young	*Lincoln: A Photobiography*
Eleanor Roosevelt: A Life of Discovery	*Martha Graham: A Dancer's Life*
Franklin Delano Roosevelt	*Out of Darkness: The Story of Louis Braille*
Immigrant Kids	*The Wright Brothers: How They Invented the Airplane*
An Indian Winter	

How do I Integrate Content Literacy Strategies into My Curriculum?

Often the first reaction of teachers to the idea of content literacy is: "I can't handle one more 'add-on' in my class. I can barely get through the content as it is." Content literacy, however, is neither an add-on to the curriculum, nor is it a substitute for content. It provides teachers and students alike with effective tools for learning the content of any subject. Teachers can increase their effectiveness in reaching more students by integrating content literacy strategies into their regular classroom instruction. Additionally, helping students to develop all of their language processes is a positive step in developing lifelong, independent learners. This independent involvement with learning can occur only when students recognize that reading and writing will empower them to change their own lives.

These are the challenges that confronted the members of the School Improvement Committee that we met at the beginning of this chapter. While they identified the problem and expressed their frustrations at their first meeting, their second meeting was focused on possible courses of action.

Margaret Hicks, an experienced high school English teacher, began the discussion. "Last summer I attended a conference on standards and assessment. A speaker who really caught my attention described the power of integrating reading and writing with content to improve student thinking. I've thought a lot about the difficulties our students have with reading and writing, and how frustrated we are with their limited thinking in our subject areas. I'm convinced that we need to help our students read and write better, and to think at higher levels, not necessarily just for better scores on tests, but so they can lead better lives."

"As teachers, we are mandated to implement content standards and improve assessment results," responded Claire Walkington, a K-12 reading specialist. "But all of these mandates are meaningless if we don't change how we approach reading and writing instruction in all subject areas and at all levels. We _can_ improve how our students learn if all teachers focus on developing content literacy in all content areas. But we have to learn new strategies and _how_ to use these strategies for teaching content literacy."

"I agree that it is important for us as classroom teachers to seek the _how_ so we can make change happen in a meaningful way," Kevin replied. "Standards and assessment by themselves are of limited value. The real question becomes: How do I respond to these mandates and implement them in my classroom in a way that really works? All the teachers I know are frustrated with the limited thinking abilities and poor reading and writing skills of their students, but we don't know how to help them. We're not reading teachers like Claire, or writing teachers like Margaret. I think we all need to know more about content literacy and especially what strategies will work in our classes to improve reading, writing, and thinking."

◆ ◆ ◆

References

Graves, M., & Graves, B. (1994). *Scaffolding reading experiences: Designs for student success.* Norwood, MA: Christopher-Gordon.

Irvin, J. L., Lunstrum, J. P., Lynch-Brown, C., & Shepard, M. F. (1995). *Enhancing social studies through literacy strategies.* Washington, DC: National Council for the Social Studies.

Manzo, A. V., & Manzo, U. (1997). *Content area literacy: Interactive teaching for active learning* (2nd edition). Upper Saddle River, NJ: Merrill.

Moore, D. W., Moore, S. A., Cunningham, P. M., & Cunningham, J. W. (1998). *Developing readers & writers in the content areas: K-12* (3rd edition). New York: Longman.

Moss, B., Leone, S., & Dipillo, M. L. (1997). Exploring the literature of fact: linking reading and writing through information trade books. *Language arts, 74* (6), 418–429.

Palmer, R. G., & Stewart, R. A. (May 1997). Nonfiction trade books in content area instruction: Realities and potential. *Journal of Adolescent and Adult Literacy, 40* (8), 630–641.

Postman, N. (1979). *Teaching as a conserving activity.* New York: Delacorte.

Vacca, R. T., & Vacca, J. A. (1996). *Content area reading* (5th edition). New York: HarperCollins.

CHAPTER 2

A Framework for Content Literacy Instruction

♦ ♦ ♦

TO: Members of the School Improvement Committee
FROM: Claire Walkington, Reading Specialist and Kevin Barkley, Middle School Science Teacher
DATE: Sept. 29
RE: Content Literacy Update

We've spent the past few weeks talking to teachers in all different subject areas and at many grade levels about content literacy. While some are ready and eager to learn, others are more cautious, and, of course, some are down-right resistant. We've also heard several recurring myths that discourage some teachers from learning how to use reading and writing as instructional tools in their content areas. We've listed several of them for discussion at our next meeting.

Myth #1 "I already use reading and writing with my textbooks. The students take turns reading the chapter aloud during class and then they answer the questions. I don't have any problems."

Myth #2 "There isn't that much reading in math books. So what would I have them write about in my math class?"

Myth #3 "Textbook reading and report writing are fine for advanced science classes, but my classes are all hands-on. I never use textbooks."

Myth #4 "The most time-efficient way to teach history [and probably many other subjects] is by lecturing. There's just too much to cover and not enough time to do it any other way, and besides, the kids won't read the textbook."

Myth #5 "My classes are performance-based. Reading and writing don't really fit in my curriculum."

Myth # 6 "I'm not an English teacher and I don't know how to teach writing."

Myth # 7   "I've already spent a lot of time planning and organizing my classes so the students will feel good about themselves. They hate to read and write. I'm not going to force any more of it on them."

The concerns and attitudes expressed by these teachers echo those we have heard from other teachers across the country. In our experience, however, these myths lose much of their power when teachers have both an instructional framework that fits their content areas and practical strategies that really work with their students. Some teachers need opportunities to discuss their beliefs about teaching and learning as they begin the difficult process of changing how they approach instruction in specific content areas. Others need to witness their colleagues' excitement and success with new methods before they are comfortable with implementing different instructional strategies. The purpose of this chapter is to help facilitate that change process by providing an instructional framework for integrating content literacy with the teaching of content. We address the following questions:

What is an instructional framework?

Why should I use an instructional framework?

What are the components of the instructional framework?

How do I make it work in my classroom?

The chapter includes an account of the personal experiences of Jon Zdrojewski, middle school math teacher, who integrated content literacy into his classroom instruction. Finally, it concludes with An Author's Perspective from Eve Bunting.

What is an Instructional Framework?

An instructional framework is a basic structure of components that describes a learning process. An instructional framework may be seen as a roadmap with benefits for both teachers and students. A roadmap is a guide, not a rigid lockstep approach or a recipe, and it may have resting places and detours along the way. Any roadmap has alternative routes; there is almost always more than one way to get from point A to point B. Teachers use an instructional framework as a planning guide, while students use it as learning guide.

We have designed this instructional framework for integrating content literacy into all classrooms based upon the following criteria: it should be simple, but not simplistic; it should be adaptable to all content areas; and it should be practical so that teachers can and will use it. Crucial to the effectiveness of any instructional framework is its generalizability. It must be applicable in a broad curricular context, not just in a particular situation or in a single content area or grade level.

Why should I use an Instructional Framework?

The roadmap analogy is useful when we look at the variety of ways in which teachers plan for instruction in their classes. Some do it by deciding upon a topic and then dividing the class time into activities designed "to cover" the topic and fill the time. Others look at the scope and sequence of concepts or skills designated for the subject, and then develop a plan for progressing through them in some orderly fashion. Still others rely on the textbook, teacher's manual, and supplementary materials to plan for instruction. In other words, teachers plan in a number of different ways; but all can benefit from an instructional framework that has the flexibility to meet their needs.

The roadmap analogy also applies to the experiences of students. Teachers present students with a roadmap (the framework) to guide them in learning the ideas, concepts, and skills of a content area and in successfully using them. This roadmap has a series of stops (the framework components described below) as students travel on their journey. Once students understand the components of the framework, how to apply it, and its value for their individual growth, they possess a significant tool to help them become more independent in their learning.

The recognition of "alternative routes, detours, and resting places" reflects a sensitivity to the differences in how students learn. Among the factors that influence how students learn are the following: prior knowledge, learning style, interest in the content, "need-to-know," and degree of difficulty of the content to be learned. Because the framework is a guide rather than a prescription, it has the flexibility to accommodate student differences. Accommodating the needs of a diverse student population is receiving heightened interest and renewed emphasis in our schools as we learn more about the concept of multiple intelligences and as the number of students with language differences and learning disabilities increases. The framework offers a workable way to meet these differences within the context of the regular curriculum and typical time constraints.

The instructional framework is based upon several principles about learning. First, learning is not discrete; it is cumulative and complementary; all new learning builds upon previous learning. Second, learning is an act of commitment and involvement. Third, learning is a thoughtful and reflective process. Irwin et al. (1995) provide a succinct description of these learning principles in action:

> Proficient learners build on and activate their background knowledge
> before reading, writing, speaking, or listening; poor learners begin
> without thinking. Proficient learners know their purpose for learning,
> give it their complete attention, and keep a constant check on their
> understanding; poor learners do not know or even consider whether or
> not they understand. Proficient learners also decide whether they have
> achieved their goal, and summarize and evaluate their thinking. (p. 5)

As both teachers and students travel along any route, they have the opportunity to pause for review or further clarification. Or they may elect to revisit ideas or concepts for increased understanding or more in-depth exploration. A framework, therefore, reflects the naturally recursive nature of the learning process. The framework, whether it is viewed as a roadmap or any other analogy, is useful only when it engages both students and teachers in mental activity to invigorate the framework. Based upon the constructivist theory, as explained by Brooks and Brooks (1993), ". . . we construct our own understandings of the world in which we live. We search for tools to help us understand our experiences" (p. 4).

What are the Components of the Instructional Framework?

The instructional framework consists of three major conceptual components: *Initiating, Constructing,* and *Utilizing*. Returning to our roadmap analogy, these are the three significant locations on any journey incorporating content literacy into a classroom. Another way of looking at this process is to use the traditional framework of pre-reading/pre-writing, during reading/during writing, and post-reading/post-writing. In keeping with the roadmap analogy, pre-reading and pre-writing may be equated to the preparations that one makes before a journey. During reading and during writing activities are those that occur on a journey to make it progress smoothly. The post-reading and post-writing activities are those in which students reflect back on their journey and apply what they have learned in new contexts. Inherent in this framework is the recognition that learning of any sort is not a lock-step experience. Learning is recursive; thus the instructional framework must be flexible enough to allow students and teachers to revisit locations during the journey. At each of the locations, *Initiating, Constructing,* and *Utilizing*, students and teachers also undergo both reflective and evaluative processes.

In the next section, we describe each of the components and the roles that students and teachers play and the experiences that they share in learning through content literacy. The first component is initiating.

Initiating

The initiating component of the instructional framework is the location where students and teachers begin, or the point of departure. Initiating is the preparatory phase; it is the stage-setting for learning. In familiar terms, it parallels the pre-reading/pre-writing stages in process learning, but it also encompasses broader processes for both teachers and students. One of the key elements of this component embraces the notion that the prior knowledge students already possess plays a major role in helping them to understand, relate, organize, and utilize new information. Activating and building upon prior knowledge are crucial to the initiating component because learning proceeds from the known to the unknown. Readance et al. (1998, p. 70) emphasize the importance of assessing prior knowledge of a topic because of its tremendous influence on the success or failure of the student in the learning experience. Essentially, most successful learning experiences begin with both evaluative and reflective processes. At times these processes are better defined and articulated than at others, but they include some form—whether informal or formal—of assessment, planning, and looking at the experience as a whole. In Chapter 3, we describe instructional strategies for initiating that also help teachers and students to assess prior knowledge.

Figure 2.1 describes the processes engaged in by both teachers and students during the initiating phase.

Teachers	Students
introduce the content	preview the content
assess prior knowledge	assess prior knowledge
spark/develop prior knowledge	activate/build prior knowledge
identify purposes and parameters	determine purposes
plan by building on prior knowledge	connect with prior knowledge
stimulate curiosity	raise questions and issues
create a need to know	recognize a need to know
develop a strategic plan for teaching	develop a strategic plan for learning

Figure 2.1

Lindsay Johnston discovered several initiating strategies to be especially useful when teaching social studies. First, she used Factstorming to activate her students' prior knowledge about immigration, stimulate their curiosity about the topic, and help them develop a strategic plan for learning more about it. The next day she wrote VocabAlert! on the board and used this strategy to help her students assess their understanding of important terms related to immigration and create a "need-to-know." Several days later she had her students do a Quick Write to reflect upon their current level of under-standing about the controversies over immigration in their own community and spark their interest in yet another aspect of this topic (see Chapter 3 for a complete description of these strategies).

The instructional framework serves as a personal roadmap for both teachers and students. At the initiating stage, they plan for active engagement in the next phase, of the learning experience, the construction of meaning.

Constructing

The initiating phase launches the constructing component of the instructional frame-work. During the constructing phase, students and teachers actively engage in devel-oping new knowledge, new understandings, and new skills. Constructing is not sim-ply a process of acquiring formation. As Beck et al. (1997) explain, "According to a constructivist view, learning cannot happen simply by getting information from a source; understanding cannot be extracted from a text and put into a student's head, nor can it be delivered to a learner" (p. 9). Learning is not a passive act in which the teacher dispenses knowledge and the student receives it. Rather it is an active process during which students build or create knowledge by constructing meaning in a variety of ways and from a variety of sources. Brooks and Brooks (1993) say that even information that we gain passively ". . . must be mentally acted upon in order to have meaning for the learner (p. 27)."

The role of the teacher in the constructing component varies greatly depending on a number of variables, including the needs of the students as indicated in the initiating component; nature and size of the class; diverse learning styles of students; complexity of the subject matter or skills; and time to be spent on a particular learning experience. Responding to the variables in the learning situation, teachers may be instructors, teaching new and complex material or they might be facilitators, helping students to discover answers and directions for themselves, or they may act in some combination of both roles. In other cases, teachers may direct student activity or serve more as a guide. Teachers may also join their students as co-learners as they seek solutions to problems or explore new concepts. In all of these situations, teachers use a variety of ways to assist student learning. Among them are the following: explaining, clarifying, elaborating, modeling, demonstrating, thinking aloud, structuring, sequencing, and providing examples and analogies. Yet another way to examine the roles of teachers is by looking at the processes that students undergo during the constructing component.

Constructing is an interactive phase in which students are actively engaged in processing what they learn and incorporating it into their schemata. For learning truly to occur, students must be active participants as they think about new information and ideas and see connections with previously learned concepts and ideas. In Figure 2.2 some of the processes that students experience in constructing are identified. These are representative rather than inclusive.

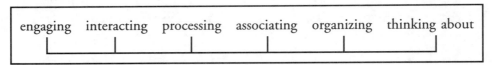

Figure 2.2 Representative Processes in Constructing

◆ ◆ ◆

Aaron Amon was frustrated because his math students would flip through the assigned textbook pages and declare that nothing made sense. Then he taught his class several pen-in-hand strategies (see Chapter 4 for a complete description) and he found that the students were actually reading the textbook and attempting to use the problem-solving procedures in it.

◆ ◆ ◆

The component of constructing occurs on two levels, with reflecting and assessing an integral part of each level. The first level occurs as students experience an immediate, basic understanding of new information. If the students are engaged in reading, this level of constructing may occur at the level of intra-sentence comprehension; that is, the understanding of a single sentence. In writing, this first level is that of functional writing or writing without composing such as notetaking and listmaking. The second level of constructing occurs when students organize and put together information, ideas, and concepts from a longer selection or from multiple sources or over a longer period of time "to see the big picture." If students are engaged in reading, the second level of constructing occurs at the level of inter-sentence comprehension as they process and organize information to form a coherent whole; this second level in writing is composing, the construction of ideas into an original whole.

It is also important to recognize how students remember what they have learned. In the process of collecting, storing, and organizing what they learn, students use what Richardson and Morgan (1997, p. 68) call "a mind blueprint" or schema. Schema theory is a description of how individuals commit to memory what they have learned. It acknowledges the significance of relevance to student learning. If students do not connect with new information or concepts, they do not add it to their mental blueprints; however, if the new learning is relevant, it taps into students' prior knowledge and they make new connections.

Reading about a topic isn't enough; listening to a lecture on a topic isn't enough; viewing a film or video on a topic isn't enough. Students need multiple opportunities to *construct* meaning: by reacting, writing, discussing, thinking about their own reactions, and responding to the reactions of others. Additionally, multiple sources of information must be available to reflect the complexity of the learning experience. Learning is not an isolated or solitary experience. Learners need to share their discoveries; they need to try out their new ideas; they need to test their assumptions. But their awareness about learning should not end there.

Students need to learn to think about their own thinking; they need to learn to recognize and understand how they learn. In this process, called *metacognition,* students develop the reflective abilities to recognize *how* they respond to learning; by doing so, they are creating the keys to unlock challenging material. Once they understand how they learn, they are able to apply this reflective process to new situations and make new learning more accessible. Students who understand how they learn are able to become strategic learners who make appropriate decisions about how to approach a learning task and create conditions and strategies that are most helpful. In Chapter 4, we describe instructional strategies for constructing that also help students become strategic learners who effectively use their metacognitive processes.

◆ ◆ ◆

Leanne Ola found that graphic organizers helped the students in her English language arts class to understand at a deeper level the novels they were reading. They used VIP maps, Venn Diagrams, and Data Charts (see Chapter 4 for a complete description of these strategies) to interact with the characters, to respond to events, and to internalize the major themes.

During the constructing component, the emphasis is upon students internalizing learning and making it their own. This internal dimension leads to the third component of the instructional framework, utilizing, during which students act upon their learning, first in familiar contexts, and then in new and different contexts.

Utilizing

The utilizing component of the instructional framework is where students begin to branch out on their own while the teacher continues to support and facilitate their learning. Utilizing serves as dual purpose learning; first, it builds upon the initiating and constructing phases; and second, it provides students with opportunities to apply or act upon the meanings they have constructed. It answers the perennial questions that students pose, "Why do we have to learn this stuff? When are we ever going to use it? What does it have to do with what's going on in our lives?"

The teacher's role during the utilizing component is multifaceted. As in the constructing phase, it is highly dependent upon the instructional variables in the existing situation. While teachers may continue to use many of the strategies they employed during the constructing phase—explaining, clarifying, modeling, demonstrating—the emphasis is less upon the teacher and more upon the student. Within this context, the teacher designates the parameters of the learning situation, but the students must then utilize their knowledge and skills to fulfill it.

Utilizing embodies a number of processes as students apply, synthesize, problem-solve, and create. Graves and Graves (1994) talk about the processes that students experience with reading that contribute to utilizing by helping students to ". . . extend ideas, to explore new ways of thinking, doing, and seeing—to invent and create, to ponder the question 'what if?'" (p.115).

Students also experience these processes when using writing during utilizing as they synthesize information, clarify and organize ideas, and create ways to communicate what they think and feel to others.

As with constructing, utilizing has levels. It is a thoughtful process in which students must use their minds as sculpting tools to chisel and refine concepts and ideas so that they are useful and relevant. In the first level, students experience ways of applying ideas to a narrow context. The second level provides students with opportunities to solve problems. Finally, when the information is used and bridged to ever-increasing and more in-depth connections, students reach a third level of utilizing. At this level, students demonstrate a high degree of independence and initiative and are able to utilize their "school learnings" beyond the context of the classroom.

◆ ◆ ◆

Julie Emerson is known as a teacher who makes science come alive. She provides her students with experiences that help them understand how much science is an integral part of their daily lives and that they can use their knowledge of science to solve significant problems. Students found that using the strategies of RAFT and ACTION with FACTS (see Chapter 5 for a complete description) helped them with the labs, projects, and writing for publication experiences.

◆ ◆ ◆

We can examine the components (initiating, constructing, utilizing) of the instructional framework on a continuum reflecting the degree of student independence. Utilizing is at the far end of the continuum, reflecting the highest degree of student independence. We must remember, also, that the ultimate goal of content literacy with this instructional framework is to help students become active, independent learners and thinkers.

It is important to note that none of the processes that students use is totally compartmentalized in one component or another. For example, one of the key processes in initiating is predicting as students anticipate the new learning experience; whereas, during constructing, predicting is useful in helping students to hypothesize about the relationship of ideas and their impact on one another. In utilizing, predicting serves as a bridge to new ideas and concepts.

While reflecting is an essential ingredient of all three components of the instructional framework, it holds special significance for the utilizing phase because students reflect not only upon this phase but also upon the entire learning experience. Reflecting provides students with an opportunity to integrate all aspects of the learning experience into a coherent whole. Reflecting can serve the function of helping students to see what they have learned and have accomplished, and additionally provide a new sense of direction. In Chapter 5, we describe instructional strategies for utilizing that include both reflecting and evaluating.

Evaluation is also a key ingredient of all three components of the instructional framework, but may serve several different functions during the utilizing component. Teachers who adhere to a constructivist philosophy of learning attempt to use some form of authentic assessment as described by Brooks & Brooks (1993), "Authentic activities (tasks and problems already relevant or of emerging relevance to students) also relate to a particular body of knowledge, but rather than structuring assessment around specific bits of information, they invite students to exhibit what they have internalized and learned through application" (pp. 96–97). Traditionally, evaluation is viewed as a paper-and-pencil procedure, usually in a multiple-choice format, conducted after instruction to assess mastery of knowledge and skills and to provide justification for letter grades and class rankings. Increasingly, states have mandated assessment procedures purported to provide a measure of the quality of the schools' programs. These high-stakes tests frequently result in driving the curriculum and determining classroom instruction. It is our belief, however, that authentic assessment is an integral part of good instruction *and* that it can have a positive impact on student performance on other forms of testing.

How do I Make it Work in My Classroom?

Effective teachers are good decision-makers. When teachers are committed to content literacy, they make strategic decisions that result in more effective teaching and heightened student involvement in learning. They do this based on understanding and implementing the concept of scaffolding. Graves and Graves (1994, p. 19) describe scaffolding as: ". . . a temporary structure that enables a person to successfully complete a task he or she could not complete without the aid of the scaffold."

Scaffolding may be likened to the process of teaching a young person to swim. Just as we would reject throwing a child into the water "to sink or swim," so we reject any notion that students do not need to have appropriate support for learning. Children learning to swim may need floatation devices as they learn how to breath in the water and develop proficiency kicking and doing the arm strokes. So learners need teachers to support their efforts as they are initiated into new ways of learning and thinking and as they begin to construct new meanings for themselves and then find ways to utilize that learning to bridge to new ideas and concepts. As with swimmers, learners are able to become increasingly independent as they progress. In both cases, the support or scaffolding can be slowly taken away as they become independent.

Our instructional framework is designed to provide students with a scaffold based on content literacy strategies that help students to become independent learners by supporting their initial experiences with new ways of learning, their efforts to build or create meaning from their experiences, and then their opportunities to use their learning in new and varied ways. Throughout this process, the need for the scaffold diminishes and students gain confidence and independence in their efforts.

The impact of scaffolding is that it helps teachers to plan strategically for instruction. A strategic teacher sets the purposes for instruction to meet the needs of the students and the standards of the content. The purposes constitute the *why* of the curriculum, whereas student needs and content are the *what*. The remaining puzzle piece is the *how,* which scaffolding addresses by establishing content learning strategies to help students to become ever-increasingly independent learners. The instructional framework provides a natural progression through which the teacher use strategies to help students make the initial connection with their learning (initiating, see Chapter 3). Once students have made this initial connection, the teacher, at the next stage of the framework, selects strategies to help students become actively involved in their learning by interacting and reacting and thinking about those responses as they internalize or build meaning (constructing, see Chapter 4). At the final phase of the framework, the need for the scaffold is diminishing because at this point the teacher recognizes that strategies should be used to help students become increasingly independent in order to find ways to use their learning (utilizing, see Chapter 5).

Scaffolding and the instructional framework we propose provide a mutually supportive structure for helping teachers to use strategies for improving student learning. They also provide for flexibility in the curriculum where literature, other printed materials, and technology can be used to increase student involvement and interest. In the final sections of this chapter, we listen to two voices: the first is of a teacher as he describes the content literacy strategies he tried and their effect on his students; the second is that of the award-winning author of children's and young adult literature, Eve Bunting.

Jon Zdrojewski, Middle School Math Teacher

I had three major content literacy goals this semester with my math classes and I feel that I have attained all of them. The first was to incorporate reading for understanding into my math classes. I have accomplished that even more than I had first hoped I would. Almost all of the math problems my students will face in the real world will be word problems, not just a list of numbers. My students now expect to read for understanding from various sources, not just the textbook. We use newspapers in class and the students have to read various advertisements and take them apart to determine if the deal is really that good. They also have become much better at solving the all too difficult word or story problems in math. I have incorporated cloze activities, we have tried listing the ten most important math words, and I have read math picture books to my classes. My students no longer ask me why they have to read in math class. They no longer try to separate the two subjects, but seem to realize that they have to read effectively to do math.

My second goal was to try some new strategies to help my students convey math concepts through writing. I feel much more comfortable using writing now with the problem-solving approach. I also know the importance of students being able to write the reasons for their answers on the state assessment test. I have, therefore, incorporated writing into every assignment by having my students write the reasoning behind their answers. I find that they seem to be more interested in doing math when they are also explaining how they got the answers. I really believe that if you can write or explain it, then you know it. I have seen this with my own eyes, and my students have seen it for themselves, too.

My final goal was to help my students see the connection of reading and math to their everyday lives. I have incorporated that concept throughout this semester using my Problem of the Day, at least to a small extent. I think that using the newspapers in my classrooms has greatly helped my students to see some connections. They are learning that they really need to be informed shoppers when they buy anything. They are at an age when money is playing a much larger role in their lives. Whenever I can relate a concept to money, I have their attention! For next semester, I plan on having my students do some research on an occupation that they would like to have in the future. They will have to tell me what education they need as well as their expected income for this position. I will then give them a job, and they will use the newspaper to find an apartment, do grocery shopping, and buy a car. They will have to use a budget and shop wisely, using the newspapers, for everything they want. I think this will be an excellent way to make connections with reading and math and real life; so do my students. They are already talking about it!

An Author's Perspective
EVE BUNTING

Eve Bunting is the author of more than 150 books for children and young adults. Born and educated in Ireland, she now lives in Pasadena, California with her husband.

Her many honors include 28 state awards, the Golden Kite, the Edgar Allan Poe Mystery Writers of America Award, and the Pen International Literary Award. Eve Bunting is the author of Smoky Night, *a Caldecott Medal winner. She is the recipient of a Jane Addams Peace Award honor book. She also received the 1997 Regina Medal and the 1999 Kerlan Award.*

I want to write books that students will enjoy reading. That is my number one priority.

Reading is such an adventure . . . an adventure you can have any time, anywhere, and at any age. How lucky can we be?

I love it when teachers realize this and pass the joy on to their students. Reading and time for reading should always be a treat. "If you finish your other work I will let you read for twenty minutes." The words spoken with a joyous smile. And blessings on teachers who read novels aloud to their classes, stopping at the perfect cliffhanger, enticing their listeners to crave the next installment!

I don't ever want to moralize in my books. But I do want to have a "truth" hidden in the pages. It may be as simple as "lying is stupid and can get you into trouble." Or as subtle as "don't give in to peer pressure if in your heart you know your peers are wrong." When the reading is over I want to have left something of value to be pondered even if not accepted.

Recently I have been doing more books set in times past. *S.O.S. Titanic,* which is about . . . well, you know what it's about. Or *Train to Somewhere,* which depicts what it was like to be an orphan in the 1800s and be shipped off—"trained off," actually—to live with and work for strangers.

Teachers "use" these kinds of books as jumping-off places for English Literature and also social studies. I admire the way their minds work and how they encourage their students to think and learn.

Often I am astonished when children write and tell me how their class planted a *Sunflower House* after they read my book of the same title. Or how they made window boxes after their teacher read *Flower Garden* to them. They will draw flower pictures for me, name the flowers, tell me their colors. They tell me when to plant them and how often to water them. They have become young gardeners! Clearly books are their own World Wide Web!

I love my work. When I write a new book I become my main character and when you read you come with me. So come! Let's go adventuring together!

<table>
<tr><td colspan="2" align="center">Selected Titles</td></tr>
<tr><td align="center">Picture Books</td><td align="center">Novels</td></tr>
</table>

Picture Books	Novels
The Blue and the Gray	*Face at the Edge of the World*
Cheyenne Again	*The Hideout*
A Day's Work	*Jumping the Nail*
Flower Garden	*S.O.S. Titanic*
Fly Away Home	*Sharing Susan*
Going Home	*Someone is Hiding on Alcatraz Island*
Smoky Night	*Spying on Miss Muller*
Sunflower House	*Such Nice Kids*
Sunshine Home	*A Sudden Silence*
Terrible Things	
Train to Somewhere	
The Wall	

References

Beck, I. L., et al. (1997). *Questioning the author: An approach for enhancing student engagement with text.* Newark, DE: International Reading Association.

Brooks, J. G., and Brooks, M. G. (1993). *In search of understanding: The case for constructivist classrooms.* Alexandria, VA: Association for Supervision and Curriculum Development.

Graves, M., & Graves, B. (1994). *Scaffolding reading experiences: Designs for student success.* Norwood, MA: Christopher-Gordon Publishers.

Irvin, J. L., et al. (1995). *Enhancing social studies through literacy strategies.* Washington, DC: National Council for the Social Studies.

Readance, J. E., Bean, T. W., & Baldwin, R. S. (1998). *Content area literacy: An integrated approach* (6th edition). Dubuque, IA: Kendall.

Richardson, J. S., & Morgan, R. F. (1997). *Reading to learn in the content areas* (3rd edition). Belmont, CA: Wadsworth.

CHAPTER 3

Strategies for Initiating

Initiating is the first component of the instructional framework. It is the preparatory phase; initiating is the launching site for the entire learning experience. Key elements of this component include activating and building upon prior knowledge, purpose-setting, creating a need to know, and stimulating curiosity. Providing opportunities for reflection and assessment during the initiating phase are also crucial to the goal of students developing both content knowledge and content literacy strategies that enable them to be lifelong learners. As the beginning point of the instructional framework, initiating provides the foundation for the more in-depth learning that takes place in the subsequent components of constructing and utilizing (see Chapter 2 for a detailed description of the entire instructional framework).

Scaffolding with Content Literacy

While the instructional framework provides a road map for improving instruction and student learning, it is important to determine *how* to implement it. Following our road map analogy, strategies are the vehicles for traveling the routes of learning described by the components of the framework (initiating, constructing, and utilizing). Effective teachers are strategic in that they understand how students learn, develop strategies to meet their diverse needs, and provide the scaffolding that helps students become independent learners. Effective students are also strategic; they build a repertoire of strategies for learning and know when, why, and how to use those strategies. In this chapter and the two following chapters, we describe strategies, provide procedures for implementing them, and present examples of how content teachers have used them. We also include the perspective of authors of young adult and children's literature.

   In the following section, award-winning author Joyce Hansen shares her thoughts on writing.

An Author's Perspective
JOYCE HANSEN

Joyce Hansen was born in The Bronx in New York City, the setting of her first three novels. She grew up with two brothers in a large and close extended family. She was a teacher and staff developer for twenty-two years in the New York City public school system. She also taught writing and literature at Empire State College, State University of New York. Now she and her husband live in South Carolina, where she writes full time.

Joyce Hansen has received several awards, including the Coretta Scott King Honor Book Award for three of her historical novels. The Captive *also received the 1994 Children's Book Award from the African Studies Association.*

Since I am a former reading teacher, I'm concerned that my own books encourage a love of reading, i.e., that reading the text is not a chore, and that the young reader will want to read other books. It doesn't matter whether they read my books or someone else's, just as long as they continue to read. I have learned so much from young people during my years of teaching and writing. One of the most important things I have learned is that the author's and the reader's imaginations must connect before anything else happens.

When I was a special education teacher, I had a student who was about fifteen years old and reading around the fifth- or sixth-grade level. In his previous classes he'd been reading only out of workbooks. I kept a collection of young adult and middle grade literature in my classroom, believing that even students who had problems reading could benefit from quality literature. I gave him the excellent book, *Felita,* by Nicholasa Mohr. My student was Puerto Rican, like the family in the book. Without introduction, I handed him the short novel, saying simply: "No more workbooks, Jose. Try this." He began to read and after about ten minutes he called out, "Oh, Miss Hansen, this is a Puerto Rican family in this book. I never read a book with Puerto Ricans in it before." He was thrilled and so was I. He'd

discovered himself in a book. His successful reading experience with *Felita* gave him confidence to pursue his interests in other books.

One of the main things I am trying to accomplish with my historical fiction and non-fiction is to make history come alive for the reader—to create characters who can wrap human emotions around the facts and figures of historical research and breathe life into them. Also, I think of my historical writing as my way of helping to eliminate the kind of stereotypes of Africans and African-Americans that I found in the books I read when I was a youngster; therefore, if my characters happen to be enslaved, they are still very much people like you and I. They fall in love, they are selfish and kind, smart and foolish, good and bad, clever and slow—in other words, they evidence a full range of human emotions and types.

In the historical as well as the contemporary fiction, I try to create characters and situations that youngsters understand. I want my readers to feel uplifted by the end of my stories and encouraged never to give up. Also, I want them to know that whenever you help someone else, you help yourself as well. A generous heart is the greatest gift.

I have also learned much from the young people who write me letters. Whenever I receive a letter from a student, I am

reminded of the great responsibility facing those of us who write for young people. We cannot afford to be careless with our pens. I also feel blessed whenever I get a	letter from a young person indicating that I have written something that either brought them joy or helped them in some way to cope with their lives.

Selected Titles

Fiction	Nonfiction
The Gift Giver	*Between Two Fires*
Yellow Bird and Me	*Breaking Ground, Breaking Silence: The*
Home Boy	*Story of New York's African Burial*
Which Way Freedom?	*Ground* (with Gary McGowan)
Out From This Place	*Women of Hope: African Americans Who*
The Captive	*Made a Difference*
I Thought My Soul Would Rise and Fly	

In our experience, we have found that highly successful teachers incorporate several ongoing organizational strategies in their classrooms that provide strong scaffolding and promote student involvement and ownership in their learning experiences. Two that seem particularly appropriate for content literacy instruction are What's My Goal? and Content Notebook/Portfolio. The discussion of these two organizational strategies will be followed by a number of instructional strategies for initiating.

What's My Goal? is an approach to goal-setting that focuses on developing both content understanding and content literacy. Used when initiating a new unit, section, or skill, it helps to establish purpose and sense of direction. Together the teacher and the students establish major categories for goal-setting such as demonstrating specific content knowledge and improving content reading, writing, or listening strategies. What's My Goal? combines both class goals and individual goals to foster student responsibility, accountability, interdependence, and independence. This approach to goal-setting helps students to reflect upon and assess their own growth. It also serves as a valuable assessment tool for teachers and can be used in conjunction with mandated standards and benchmarks.

Content Notebook/Portfolio is a valuable organizational device that also can serve as an assessment tool. Structured in a variety of ways depending upon variables such as subject, grade, and curriculum, course notebooks can be used to house ongoing and daily work or can be turned into assessment portfolios that provide a record of student progress. Whether serving as a notebook or portfolio, these devices should be introduced during the initiating component of the instructional framework to help students focus, plan, and organize their learning. Notebooks/portfolios are then used regularly in all of the components. Among the sections frequently included are: goals, assignments, assignment calendar, vocabulary, class notes, reading responses, projects, labs, group work, reflections, and evaluation record.

The remainder of the chapter presents teaching strategies for the initiating component of the instructional framework. The strategies are designed to be adapted and used in most content area classrooms. While most teachers will use these strategies with printed materials, many of them are adaptable to films and videos, also. Students' visual literacy can be enhanced greatly through the use of strategies that help them engage in active learning rather than passive viewing.

STRATEGY: Content Journal

Component:	Content Literacy Process:	Organizing for Instruction:
Initiating	Reading	Individual
Constructing	Writing	Pairs
Utilizing	Speaking	Small Group
	Listening	Whole Class
	Viewing	

Description:

A content (substitute a class title, e.g., Algebra) journal is one that teachers have their students keep as an on-going record of their progress in the class. The essential purpose for the content journal is to have students interact regularly with course content. As an initiating strategy, the content journal provides students with opportunities to become personally engaged in the learning of content. Content journals are among the most flexible tools for achieving student involvement because they can be used in a number of ways, including fostering student reflection. Having students briefly recap and reflect on new learning helps with both clarification of questions and retention of unfamiliar concepts. A content journal may be used at any time in or out of class as teachers provide students with opportunities to interact with new and challenging ideas. The important element of the content journal is that entries always have a content focus. A variety of purposes and times for using the content journal makes it more effective than using a set schedule and format.

Procedures:

- Students either have a loose leaf or spiral notebook, 8½ x 11, that they bring to class each day. (Some teachers find it advantageous to have the content journals left in the classroom).
- Students always respond to a specific writing prompt in the content journals; for example: defining a key term in their own words; describing their reaction to something in the lesson; explaining a concept in their own words; assessing their understanding of specific content; providing examples to illustrate a point.
- Students respond to the prompts in 5–10 minutes.
- The emphasis on assessment of the journals should be on their usefulness for the students.

Variations:

- One of the most effective variations of the content journal is using it when the teacher perceives confusion among students. When new and difficult concepts are introduced, students will differ in how quickly they grasp the new material. An effective way in which some teachers use the content journal is to stop immediately when students seem confused. Then they have the students write what they have just learned. The teacher spot checks to see where students are having problems. The teacher can immediately either clarify or reteach the confusing material (Brown, Phillips, and Stephens, 1993, p. 77).

- Some teachers have journal writing on a specific schedule, daily or three times a week. They also have set assignments that students do in their journals.

- Teachers in math and science often have students apply a problem-solving process or make up a word problem and solve it in their content journals.

Examples:

Karen Roberts uses content journals in her Spanish 2 class to have students practice vocabulary and sentence construction by writing dialogues in their journals.

In her math classes, Jane Collins uses journals to have her students raise questions about the problems that they do. For each homework set, she has students write specific questions. The questions become the basis for the initial class activity and reteaching.

STRATEGY: Brainstorming

Component:	Content Literacy Process:	Organizing for Instruction:
Initiating	Reading	Individual
Constructing	Writing	Pairs
Utilizing	Speaking	Small Group
	Listening	Whole Class
	Viewing	

Description:

"Brainstorming is a process of generating as many ideas as possible without initially doing any refinement or evaluation" (Brown, Phillips, & Stephens, 1993, p. 101). The emphasis is upon encouraging students to activate their prior knowledge and make connections. Brainstorming creates a bridge between what students already know and the topic being initiated. It also provides teachers with a quick, informal assessment of student familiarity and background knowledge. When included in the utilizing component of the instructional framework, brainstorming is used to promote problem-solving and divergent thinking.

Procedures:

- The teacher presents a prompt to the class for brainstorming.
- Students generate responses.
- Responses are recorded so that all may read them.
- Additional responses are generated and recorded.
- The teacher engages the class in discussion about the responses and uses them as a springboard to the new lesson content.

Variations:

- Some teachers establish parameters for brainstorming, such as a minimum number of responses each student must generate or other appropriate conditions.
- Some teachers use a series of short brainstorming prompts sequenced to heighten student curiosity about the lesson content.
- After the students generate responses to the brainstorming prompt, they write a brief statement predicting the focus of the new lesson.
- Brainstorming is almost always a group process, however, some teachers have individuals or pairs brainstorm first, followed by group or whole class brainstorming.

Examples:

Upon entering the classroom, students examine a photograph of Abraham Lincoln and a collection of books written about him. Their social studies teacher, Griffin Scott, organizes them into small groups where they brainstorm and record their responses on large chart paper to the prompt, "Lincoln's Major Accomplishments." As a whole class, they discuss the responses and add to them. Mr. Scott then helps them organize and condense the responses into five major topics. Each group selects one area to research and present to the class.

Grace Morales, science teacher, writes the brainstorm prompt, "acid rain," on the chalkboard. First in pairs and then as a whole class, students brainstorm and record all the associations they have with the term. Next, Ms. Morales circles key responses and uses them as lead-in to a CD-ROM about the environment and then a lab demonstration.

STRATEGY: Brainracing

Component:	Content Literacy Process:	Organizing for Instruction:
Initiating Constructing Utilizing	Reading Writing Speaking Listening Viewing	Individual Pairs Small Group Whole Class

Description:

Brainracing (Brown, Phillips, and Stephens, 1993) is a process for individual students to generate as many ideas as they can on a teacher-selected topic. Brainracing is made up of three stages: recall, question, and speculate (RQS). It begins with a broad topic that students narrow down by focusing on one aspect of it. Students look in-depth at that aspect by raising questions about it and then speculating about possible answers to those questions. Using some of the idea-generating processes of brainstorming and factstorming, brainracing begins as a process of recalling as many ideas or facts about the topic as possible.

Procedures:

- Students list on paper as many ideas about the topic as they can recall in a set amount of time, such as 5–10 minutes.
- Students have a short review time to go over their lists and make any changes.
- Students select one item from their list that intrigues them.
- They then generate a list of everything that they know about that item.
- Their second list becomes the springboard for students to question what they want to learn about the topic they have selected.
- Students speculate about the answers to the questions that they have raised.
- As the class study progresses, students revisit their questions and speculations.

Variation:

- Some teachers have students use this strategy in pairs.

Example:

David Black was surprised that his middle school students were either uninformed or in some cases misinformed about the Holocaust. He used brainracing as a way of having students identify their initial impressions.

STRATEGY: Quick Write

Component:	Content Literacy Process:	Organizing for Instruction:
Initiating	Reading	Individual
Constructing	Writing	Pairs
Utilizing	Speaking	Small Group
	Listening	Whole Class
	Viewing	

Description:

A quick write is short, focused writing in response to a specific prompt. As an initiating strategy, a quick write helps to activate students' prior knowledge and provide a starting point for a lesson. A quick write serves as a bridge to the new concepts or ideas that students will be learning. It can help students see connections between previous learning experiences and the present one. While generally not graded, students' responses can be used as an informal assessment tool.

Procedures:

- The teacher formulates a statement or a question related to the content for students to respond to within a specified amount of time, usually 5–7 minutes.
- The students are told that the purpose is for them to express their thoughts and ideas without concern for the mechanics of writing.
- When the time limit expires, students share their responses with a partner and then with the whole class for discussion.

Variations:

- One variation that teachers sometimes use is to have students write for about three minutes and then exchange their papers with a learning partner who reads the paper and then continues responding where the author left off.
- Some teachers use quick writes at the end of a lesson or class period as a form of student reflection.

Examples:

Sheri Goldsmith started class by having her students do a quick write on the artist whose work they like best. Midway through the lesson, she had them do one on the artists whose work they liked the least.

In his advanced math class, Marc Tisdale uses a quick write as a check for understanding of the previous night's homework. He finds that having students describe in words the procedures for solving problems indicates how well they understand what they have been doing.

STRATEGY: Free Writing

Component:	Content Literacy Process:	Organizing for Instruction:
Initiating	Reading	Individual
Constructing	Writing	Pairs
Utilizing	Speaking	Small Group
	Listening	Whole Class
	Viewing	

Description:

"Free writing is an unstructured approach that allows students to generate their own ideas in rapid fashion without the constraints of predetermined concepts of structure and form" (Brown, Phillips, and Stephens, 1993, pp. 64–65). The term *free* is used because the writing is not limited to a specific topic and it is seldom evaluated for a grade. Free writing is a process of having students write about anything, thus exploring what they know about it. Free writing stimulates student curiosity, especially for those students who are reluctant to write. Free writing should be used only in specific contexts that acknowledge its limited focus. Free writing serves as a positive focusing strategy for students because they are allowed time to examine what they know about a topic.

Procedures:

- In doing free writing, the teacher allows the students to choose what they will write about.
- Teachers have students spend approximately 5 minutes free writing.
- Students are told to write (without stopping) for the duration of the time.
- Students may choose to share their writing at the conclusion.

Variation:

- Generally free writing is used by teachers for a limited period of time to help students overcome their aversion to writing. They then use other strategies that provide more of a content focus.

Examples:

In his American History class, John Oliver occasionally has his students begin class by doing a free write for the first 5–7 minutes of class. He follows it by a sharing period in which students may elect to either read what they have written or talk about it. He has found that many of his students use these free writes to raise questions about their reading or other class materials. Their observations serve as a springboard for class discussion.

Roberto Jaime has music playing when his students enter the room. The students do free writing for 5 minutes; they may write about how the music makes them feel or what it makes them think of or anything else they want to express in writing that day.

STRATEGY: **Mysterious Possibilities**

Component:	Content Literacy Process:	Organizing for Instruction:
Initiating Constructing Utilizing	Reading Writing Speaking Listening Viewing	Individual Pairs Small Group Whole Class

Description:

Mysterious Possibilities is a short, quick strategy intended to capture student interest, focus attention, and arouse curiosity. Incorporating elements of group brainstorming and predicting, it is particularly useful when students have little prior knowledge about a topic or question the relevance of it.

Procedures:

- With an air of mystery, the teacher shows an object, photograph, picture, or some other form of visual stimuli.
- Students are asked to solve the mystery by brainstorming and predicting possible connection to a specific topic.
- The teacher engages the class in discussion and uses the generated list of ideas as a springboard to the new lesson content.

Variations:

- As the students generate and list ideas, they explain each possible connection.
- Teachers may read a short passage, show a brief video clip, or play part of a recording in place of or in conjunction with the visual stimuli.
- Some teachers extend this strategy to the utilizing component of the instructional framework by having students create their own mysterious possibilities presentation, display, or poster.

Examples:

Joe Levine uses Mysterious Possibilities in a unit on art appreciation with his beginning art classes as he introduces Abstract Art. Students try to determine what the
subject of the painting is by brainstorming. He sometimes does a variation by listing
the titles of paintings on the board and has the students match the paintings to their
mysterious titles.

Evelyn Cooper displayed a large, twisted stop sign in the front of her classroom.
First, she had the class brainstorm their own associations with it. Then she wrote on
the board the title of a young adult novel, *Driver's Ed,* by Caroline Cooney, and
asked the students to brainstorm the possible connections between the book and the
twisted stop sign.

STRATEGY: I'm Curious . . .

Component:	Content Literacy Process:	Organizing for Instruction:
Initiating	Reading	Individual
Constructing	Writing	Pairs
Utilizing	Speaking	Small Group
	Listening	Whole Class
	Viewing	

Description:

In this strategy, students are given the opportunity to speculate about what they will be learning. The teacher briefly introduces a new topic or unit to create initial student interest. The introduction should be evocative enough to activate prior knowledge and to intrigue students to think about what the topic or unit is about.

Procedures:

- The teacher introduces a new topic or unit by name, descriptive phrase, visual image, or any means that is evocative.
- The teacher asks the students to think about what makes them curious about it.
- Then each student generates a list of at least three responses to the question: "What makes you curious about _____?"
- The lists are used as springboards to initiate the topic or unit.

Variation:

- In another variation, teachers use film or video clips, or computer images to pique student curiosity.

Example:

Darrell MacGregor introduced a unit on genetics by showing a picture of a boy with one blue eye and one brown eye, a sign that had Mendel's Law printed on it, and a chart with xs and os on it. He asked, "What makes you curious about this?"

STRATEGY: What's in a Picture?

Component:	Content Literacy Process:	Organizing for Instruction:
Initiating	Reading	Individual
Constructing	Writing	Pairs
Utilizing	Speaking	Small Group
	Listening	Whole Class
	Viewing	

Description:

This strategy is designed to use students' visual literacy to activate their prior experiences and bridge to new content. Photography can present the familiar in unfamiliar ways by using extreme close ups, cropped shots that remove the context, or even telephoto shots. Images can be deceptive and teachers can capitalize on that by using abstract images to heighten student interest and imagination by having them guess about the picture. Using the images as writing prompts, teachers can tap students' insight and imagination. Students speculate about what they are seeing in their journals.

Procedures:

- The teacher selects abstract visual images (slides, still photos, videos, or computer-enhanced graphics) that capture course concepts.
- Students view the images and try to determine what they are.
- Students complete a response guide (see Figure 3.1) in their journals.

Variations:

- Have students work in pairs, one looking at a picture, describing it to the other. The second student will make a list of what the picture may be.

- Teacher may use any sensory experience as a writing prompt to initiate student interest. For example, have students touch objects in a bag and try to guess what they are.

Response Guide

Briefly describe the image:

What does it remind you of?

Speculate what the image is and how it is connected to the lesson.

Figure 3.1

Examples:

In biology class, Diane Welch uses photographs of microscopic slides to introduce the unit on cells and their division. She has the students speculate about what is happening in the slides.

Frank Norton collects sounds. He has tapes and recordings of hundreds of sound effects and sounds of natural phenomena. He uses some of the sounds in his creative writing class as prompts for students to write descriptive passages.

STRATEGY: Question of the Day

Component:	Content Literacy Process:	Organizing for Instruction:
Initiating	Reading	Individual
Constructing	Writing	Pairs
Utilizing	Speaking	Small Group
	Listening	Whole Class
	Viewing	

Description:

Question of the Day (Hemmerich et al., 1994) is an open-ended question designed to intrigue students and activate their prior knowledge. Teachers, especially of science and math, have found the Question of the Day a good way to involve students and to help them see the relevance of what they are learning.

Procedures:

- The teacher writes the Question of the Day on the board or overhead projector. The question must be stimulating and not require a literal or simple yes/no answer; it should encourage problem-solving and creativity.
- Students respond in writing to the question. In some cases, students may want to accompany their answers with a drawing or diagram.
- Then the teacher uses their responses as a basis for class discussion and as a springboard to the day's lesson. Student responses generally are not collected and graded.

Variations:

- Students, individually, in pairs, or in small groups, can also generate the Question of the Day.
- The Question of the Day may be used prior to viewing a film or video. In this case, students respond to it after the viewing.

Example:

Lisa Branson posed this Question of the Day with her class: How are ballet and geometry alike? The students wrote in their content journals for five minutes and then discussed their responses with the whole class. Later, in small groups, they drew diagrams to illustrate the geometric shapes of various ballet positions.

STRATEGY: Clustering

Component:	Content Literacy Process:	Organizing for Instruction:
Initiating	Reading	Individual
Constructing	Writing	Pairs
Utilizing	Speaking	Small Group
	Listening	Whole Class
	Viewing	

Description:

Clustering is a process for arranging and structuring concepts to show their relation-ships. Clustering is the umbrella term for a graphic organizer that may be called mapping or webbing. It provides students with opportunities to assess their prior knowledge. This strategy is useful in helping students to gain a basic awareness of a topic and the ideas related to it.

Procedures:

- The teacher models clustering with the class by putting a topic on the board and having the students, as a group, generate ideas related to it.
- The topic is circled and the ideas that are generated are connected by lines to the topic.
- As new words are added, students group or cluster them to create a structure showing some type of relationship among the ideas.

Variations:

- Teachers often develop variations of clustering based on their content area. For example, one history teacher does clustering based on significant dates and has students add events and notable figures as they learn about the time period.
- Clusterings may be used as a notetaking device with films and videos.

Example:

Carl Yamamota uses clustering in his social studies classes to activate students' prior knowledge. He begins the cluster with a word, date, or idea central to the lesson or a new unit and then has the class add to the cluster both in content and in structure. See the example from his class shown in Figure 3.2.

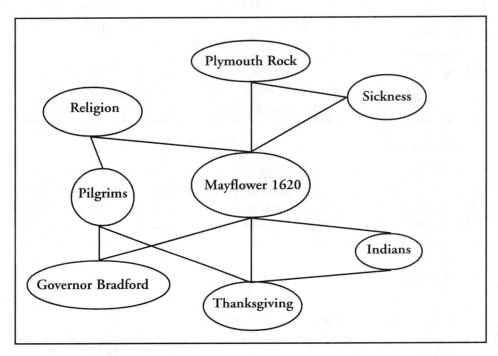

Figure 3.2 Social Studies Cluster

STRATEGY: Factstorming

Component:	Content Literacy Process:	Organizing for Instruction:
Initiating Constructing Utilizing	Reading Writing Speaking Listening Viewing	Individual Pairs Small Group Whole Class

Description:

Factstorming is similar to brainstorming, but focuses only on factual information (Richardson & Morgan, 1997). It involves students drawing upon their prior knowledge to generate facts they associate with a given topic. Our adaptation of factstorming goes a step further by engaging students in finding evidence to support their facts. Factstorming can be a useful assessment tool, helping teachers to identify gaps in student knowledge and misconceptions.

Procedures:

- The teacher presents a prompt to the class for factstorming.
- Individually, in pairs, or in small groups, students generate and record facts.
- The teacher engages the class in discussion about the responses and uses them as a springboard to the new lesson content.
- Students read to find evidence to support the facts they generated or to correct any misinformation they originally recorded. They also record new facts and evidence to support them.

Variations:

- The class develops a master list of verified facts on the lesson content.
- Some teachers have students use a two-column chart labeled Facts and Evidence.
- Students use the master list of verified facts in application activities or to solve specific problems.
- Factstorming may be used with videos and films, also.

Examples:

On the first day of class in Gloria Matson's French 1 class, she has posters of France around the room. She uses factstorming to have her students recall all that they know about the country, the geography, and the culture of France. She builds on their prior knowledge by showing a video from her last trip to Paris and the French countryside, relating to the information that they had generated during factstorming.

Molly Hyatt's class uses factstorming when they study states and geographical regions. They found a variety of print sources, but also discovered a wealth of information on the Internet to use as evidence to support their facts.

STRATEGY: K-W-L

Component:	Content Literacy Process:	Organizing for Instruction:
Initiating	Reading	Individual
Constructing	Writing	Pairs
Utilizing	Speaking	Small Group
	Listening	Whole Class
	Viewing	

Description:

Originally developed by Donna Ogle (1986), KWL is a widely used strategy designed to foster active reading. The basic three-steps consist of: K—What do I already know?, W—What do I want to know?, and L—What did I learn? KWL provides a structure for activating and building prior knowledge, for eliciting student input when establishing purposes for reading, and for personalizing the summarization of what was learned. A completed KWL chart (see Figure 3.3) can help students reflect upon and evaluate their learning experience. KWL also serves as a useful assessment tool for teachers.

Procedures:

- The teacher introduces KWL and models how to use it with a new topic or new reading selection.
- Individually, in pairs, or in small groups, students brainstorm what they already know about the topic.
- This information is recorded and displayed for the whole class. During class discussion, the teacher models how to organize and categorize information.
- The teacher leads the class into the next phase, during which students generate a list of what else they want to learn or questions they want answered. Again the teacher models how to organize and categorize their responses and how to use this information to set purposes for their reading.
- Students then read with the purpose of discovering information to answer the questions they generated.
- This information is recorded and displayed. Again the teacher models how to reflect upon the entire learning experience.

Variations:

- Some teachers slightly rephrase the first step to emphasize the tentative nature of what we remember: K—What do I think I already know? or What do I think I remember? Others leave the original wording intact, but surround the K with large question marks.
- Frequently, middle school and high school teachers get better responses from students when they change the W to N so the sequence becomes KNL, with the N representing: What do I *need* to know?
- Some teachers add a planning step, so the sequence becomes KWHL, with the H representing: How am I going to learn (or research or investigate)? or How will I express what I learn?
- Other teachers add an additional step at the end of the sequence: KWLL, with the final L representing: What do I still need to learn (or research or investigate)?
- Still another variation is to add U at the end of the sequence: KWLU, with the U representing: How can I use (apply) this information?

Examples:

Sample Charts

What I Already Know	What I Want to Know	What I Learned

Figure 3.3

K	N	L

K	W	H	L

Figure 3.4

STRATEGY: Reaction Guide

Component:	Content Literacy Process:	Organizing for Instruction:
Initiating	Reading	Individual
Constructing	Writing	Pairs
Utilizing	Speaking	Small Group
	Listening	Whole Class
	Viewing	

Description:

Sometimes called prediction or anticipation guides, reaction guides provide students with a series of statements to respond to before reading a new selection. Students respond based on their prior knowledge and previous experiences. Reaction guides help to create a need-to-know and provide a purpose for learning new information. Our adaptation of reaction guides goes a step further by engaging students in finding evidence to support their responses. While the initial responses on reaction guides should not be graded by the teacher, they can be a useful assessment device to identify gaps in student knowledge and misconceptions.

Procedures:

- The teacher creates a reaction guide by writing a series of statements, usually 3 to 7, based on important points, major concepts, controversial ideas, or misconceptions from the material the students will be reading. The statements should require students to think beyond a literal level of comprehension. (See Figure 3.5.)

- The teacher directs the students to respond to each statement based on what they currently think or believe; they will respond again after reading and have an opportunity to change their original responses. Students indicate their reactions by using agree/disagree, yes/no, true/false, correct/incorrect, or some other designation. "I don't know" is not an acceptable response—students must make an educated guess.

- Without revealing the accurate responses, the teacher uses the statements as a basis for class discussion to stimulate student curiosity and to probe the thinking behind their first responses. The teacher may also have the students who disagree with a statement predict what they think the correct information is.

- Next, students read the new material. Afterwards they respond again to the statements on the reaction guide. Then they find evidence from the new material to support their responses.

- Finally, the teacher leads a class discussion to clarify and expand upon the statements and responses.

Variations:

- Some teachers allow students to mark "I'm not sure" for their first response to statements on the reaction guide. These students, however, must locate and record specific information from the new material to support their second responses.
- A reaction guide can feature a single, key word (e.g., Roosevelt, photosynthesis, geometry) followed by a list of terms that might describe it, be associated with it, or serve as examples of it. The students mark each term on the list with T/F before reading, and then respond again after reading.
- Some teachers let students use the reaction guide while they read the new material, while others collect it and then return it to be used afterwards.
- Reaction guides may also be used in conjunction with films and videos.

Example:

Bill Southworthy uses reaction guides on a regular basis with his science classes. He finds it helps to identify his students' misconceptions on a topic. His students like reaction guides because it gives them a purpose and structure for reading their difficult textbook. When Bill creates a reaction guide, he makes sure that the statements make his students think at higher levels. While reading the text will help the students determine if the statements are accurate or inaccurate, none of the answers can be found in the text in the exact same words.

	Sample Reaction Guide, *Agree/Disagree;* The Brain and Memory	
Before Reading		*After Reading*
	1. Scientists use data from both living and dead subjects to conduct research on memory. Evidence:_____ 2. Aging seems to have a relatively minor effect on forgetfulness. Evidence:_____ 3. Alcohol abuse and Alzheimer's are major causes of memory loss. Evidence:_____	

Figure 3.5

STRATEGY: Vocab Alert!

Component:	Content Literacy Process:	Organizing for Instruction:
Initiating	Reading	Individual
Constructing	Writing	Pairs
Utilizing	Speaking	Small Group
	Listening	Whole Class
	Viewing	

Description:

Vocab Alert! is designed to make students aware of important terms prior to reading a selection. Insufficient vocabulary knowledge is a serious obstacle for many students. Frequently they skip over unfamiliar words, and thus fail to understand fully what they read. Vocab Alert! serves as a form of self-assessment for students and helps them to set purposes for their reading. It also can function as an assessment tool for teachers, helping them to determine how much vocabulary instruction and practice will be needed.

Procedure:

- The teacher selects the most important terms from the reading selection, being careful to limit them to a manageable number (5–9), and prepares a Vocab Alert! form (see Figure 3.6).
- The teacher writes Vocab Alert! on the board and the students assess their familiarity with each term using the form.
- Then the teacher introduces the significance of the terms on the form within the context of the current topic and prepares the students for the reading selection.
- As the students read the selection, they pay special attention to the Vocab Alert! terms and record information about them on the form.
- Afterwards, using their Vocab Alert! Forms, the teacher engages the class in discussion to further clarify and develop their understanding of the terms.

Variations:

- Some teachers have students designate a section of their content notebook or portfolio for vocabulary where students keep their completed "Vocab Alert!" forms.
- Some teachers use a Word Wall where they display the important Vocab Alert! terms.

Example:

I know	It's sort of familiar	Don't know

| 1 | 2 | 3 | 4 | 5 |

List of Words

1. embargo

   Notes: govt. restricts trade; see p. 356

2. treaty

   Notes: agreement bet. nations; see p. 359

3. _____

   Notes:

Figure 3.6

STRATEGY: 4-Square Vocabulary Approach

Component:	Content Literacy Process:	Organizing for Instruction:
Initiating	Reading	Individual
Constructing	Writing	Pairs
Utilizing	Speaking	Small Group
	Listening	Whole Class
	Viewing	

Description:

Adapted from the work of Eeds and Cockrum (1985), the 4-square vocabulary approach provides an interactive way to introduce key vocabulary words. Based on verbal and visual associations, it helps students draw on their prior knowledge and personal experiences to develop conceptual understanding of important content terms. Initially this strategy may seem time-consuming; however, once students have internalized it, the teacher's presentation time is greatly reduced. Then students are able to do much of it independently.

Procedures:

- The teacher directs the class to divide their paper into four squares (sections) and number each section (see Figure 3.7).
- In square 1, the students write the key vocabulary term. If the word is unfamiliar, they practice pronouncing it. Then the teacher presents the word in context and explains its definition, accompanied by verbal and visual examples and non-examples.
- Next the teacher engages the students in generating and discussing their own verbal and visual examples of the term. Then in square 2, each student writes an example from personal experience that fits the term.
- Directing their attention to square 3, the teacher engages the students in generating and discussing their own verbal and visual non-examples of the term. Each student writes a non-example from personal experience that fits the term.
- Finally, in square 4, students write a definition of the term using their own words. Then they check their definition with the dictionary or textbook glossary and refine it, if necessary. They also locate the term within the context of their reading material.

Variations:

- Some teachers also have students draw a visual representation of the term in square 4.
- When it fits the content, teachers may have students write formulas and symbols in the appropriate boxes (see Figure 3.8).
- Some teachers have changed the 4-square approach slightly so that a definition is written in square 1 and a picture, formula, or graphic in square 4 (see the math example below).
- After students clearly understand the 4-square approach, some teachers have students use it individually, in pairs, or in small groups and then present their word to the whole class.
- Some teachers have students collect their 4-square sheets in the vocabulary section of their course notebook or portfolio.

Examples:

(square 1) compromise compromised compromising	(square 2) Sometimes people have to settle things by giving up something they want. Some government delegates had to agree to give up some things they wanted to each an agreement.
(square 3) The fighting couple could not settle their differences and so they divorced. An agreement between the two countries was not reached, and so a war was started.	(square 4) A compromise is an agreement between two or more people or groups where both must give up something.

Figure 3.7 Social Studies

(square 1) Circle Set of points equal distance from a fixed point	(square 2) doughnuts wheels bowl
(square 3) box TV Washington Monument	(square 4)

Figure 3.8 Math

STRATEGY: The 10 Most Important Words

Component:	Content Literacy Process:	Organizing for Instruction:
Initiating	Reading	Individual
Constructing	Writing	Pairs
Utilizing	Speaking	Small Group
	Listening	Whole Class
	Viewing	

Description:

The 10 Most Important Words is designed to help students become aware of the value of key concepts in developing content knowledge. Frequently, students view content classes as a series of isolated, fragmented lessons, failing to see how key concepts provide the connections. This strategy fosters an understanding of the importance of prior knowledge and helps students to see the connections among various topics within a content area. It can be used prior to reading a specific selection or during the initiating phase of a unit; it can also be used again at the conclusion for reflection or evaluation.

Procedures:

- The teacher introduces a topic to the class and engages them in discussion designed to help them think about what they already know and activate their prior knowledge.
- Students are asked individually to predict and list what they think the 10 most important words or phrases in the reading selection or unit will be.
- Then students in pairs or small groups compare their lists, discussing why they selected each word. Next, each pair or small group develops a list of the 10 most important words.
- Students then read the pertinent material, paying special attention to key concepts.
- Next, each pair or group revises their original list. They must also create a graphic organizer showing the relationships of the words to each other and develop a written rationale for their final list.

Variations:

- While the strategy specifies 10 words, a smaller number can be designated just as effectively by the teacher.
- Some teachers help students develop criteria for selecting the most important words. The criteria helps students understand what the key concepts are.
- Some teachers ask students to list the 10 most important words in a specific content area, such as math or geography.

Example:

Roy Sylvester has his economics class do a stock market simulation. On the first day of the unit, he distributes a list of thirty terms that are related to the topic and tells the students that ten of them are the most important ones in successfully completing the simulation. In pairs or small groups, the students discuss and decide which ten they think are the key terms. Then the lists are posted and discussed by the entire class. The lists are referred to and revised again at the conclusion of the simulation.

STRATEGY: Word Bank

Component:	Content Literacy Process:	Organizing for Instruction:
Initiating	Reading	Individual
Constructing	Writing	Pairs
Utilizing	Speaking	Small Group
	Listening	Whole Class
	Viewing	

Description:

The word bank is a collection of words organized around a common theme, topic, or unit. As the teacher introduces the new unit, topic, or theme, students are asked what terms they can recall that are related to the topic. Contributing to the word bank activates students' prior knowledge and each contribution triggers additional terms that expand the initial word bank.

Procedures:

- The teacher explains the concept of a word bank.
- The teacher presents a new topic to the class.
- The teacher models adding words to a word bank.
- Students begin brainstorming terms that they recognize as being related to the topic.
- Each new word is written on a 5" x 7" index card, with a definition written on the back.
- As the class learns more about the topic, new vocabulary is added to the word bank.

Variation:

- A variation of the word bank is the word wall, where the words are displayed on a classroom wall as they are collected.

Example:

Carrie Soames had a word bank in her natural science class. When the class begins a new unit on Rocks and Fossils, they brainstorm the words (and their definitions) that they associate with the topic. New words and their definitions are added throughout the unit.

STRATEGY: Analogies

Component:	Content Literacy Process:	Organizing for Instruction:
Initiating	Reading	Individual
Constructing	Writing	Pairs
Utilizing	Speaking	Small Group
	Listening	Whole Class
	Viewing	

Description:

An analogy provides a familiar context for learning by presenting a comparison of something that is known with new, unfamiliar ideas or concepts. The familiar context of the analogy should be one that students can identify with and understand. Analogies work especially well during the initiating phase of the learning experience because they have strong interest value, provide a preview of what is to learned, and make abstract concepts seem less formidable.

Procedures:

- The teacher presents several analogies related to a concept and models how they are developed.
- From a list supplied by the teacher, the students—usually in pairs or small groups—choose a concept to develop an analogy.
- Students explore the concept and record its elements or characteristics.
- Next, they find a familiar concept that has elements or characteristics that are roughly parallel to the concept. They develop the analogy and present it to the class.

Variations:

- Some teachers help students learn to use analogies by presenting both parts of the comparison and then having students develop the analogy. For example, a teacher might ask a government class how a hockey game is like diplomatic negotiations. The students then develop the extended comparison.
- Some teachers use paired analogies (e.g., dog:cage as turtle:shell) to help students develop an understanding of vocabulary relationships.
- Some teachers have students draw cartoons or other visual representations to accompany the analogies.

Example:

As a physical education/health teacher, Beth Cooper was interested in the number of sports analogies that politicians were using in a recent campaign. She had her students "collect" the analogies that they heard. She had them look at the message that they sent about sports. Then she had the class develop their own analogies using sports compared with health concepts.

STRATEGY: Find Someone Who . . .

Component:	Content Literacy Process:	Organizing for Instruction:
Initiating Constructing Utilizing	Reading Writing Speaking Listening Viewing	Individual Pairs Small Group Whole Class

Description:

Find Someone Who . . . is an interactive strategy that provides students with a highly motivating format for activating prior knowledge. Students respond to each other based on a series of prompts on a specific topic. This strategy gives students a purpose for verbalizing their understanding of a topic.

Procedures:

- The teacher prepares a Find Someone Who . . . form (see Figure 3.9) by dividing a sheet of paper into six or eight boxes and writing a statement in each box. The statements relate to content the students are learning. Each box also has a place for comments and a signature.
- The teacher gives the class a specific amount of time to interact with each other with the goal of finding a different person to sign each box.
- Afterwards students share their findings with the whole class, and the teacher uses them as a springboard for the day's lesson.

Variations:

- While many teachers use this strategy to initiate a topic, others use it as a review and as a quick, informal assessment device that helps both the teacher and students determine their level of understanding on given topic.
- Some teachers design the Find Someone Who . . . form so that students must find specific facts or evidence from their textbook or other reading material to support their responses (see Figure 3.10). This approach provides a functional means for helping students to use their texts as resources and for getting them to selectively reread complex or technical material.

Examples:

FIND SOMEONE WHO . . .	
. . . can define kinetic energy. Comments: Signature:	. . . can give an example of kinetic energy. Comments: Signature:
. . . can tell the difference between convection and conduction. Comments: Signature:	. . . know what type of heating system the school has. Comments: Signature:
. . . read today's assignment! Comments: Signature:	. . . can define solar energy. Comments: Signature:
. . . knows a place that uses solar energy for heating. Comments: Signature:	. . . can give an example of hydroelectric energy. Comments: Signature:

Figure 3.9

USING YOUR GEOGRAPHY TEXTBOOK, FIND SOMEONE WHO . . .	
. . . can list the countries of South America. Pg. #: Answer: Signature:	. . . can locate the highest mountain in South America. Pg. #: Answer: Signature:
. . . can compare the population of Brazil with that of Ecuador. Pg. #: Answer: Signature:	. . . can tell you a fact they find interesting about South America. Pg. #: Answer Signature:
. . . can describe why the seasons in South America are opposite from those in North America. Pg. #: Answer: Signature:	. . . can determine which country in South America has the most valuable natural resources. Pg. #: Answer: Signature:

Figure 3.10

STRATEGY: The Two-Minute Preview

Component:	Content Literacy Process:	Organizing for Instruction:
Initiating	Reading	Individual
Constructing	Writing	Pairs
Utilizing	Speaking	Small Group
	Listening	Whole Class
	Viewing	

Description:

The Two-Minute Preview provides students with an overview of the selection and helps them develop a strategic plan for reading it. Too often students jump into a reading assignment without adequate preparation and then fail to comprehend or remember what they read. Previewing can help students assume an active stance, particularly with difficult, complex, or highly technical material. To be effective, teachers should model several different ways of previewing and provide students with ongoing practice.

Procedures:

- The teacher provides the class with a brief outline or checklist for previewing (see Figure 3.11). The outline or checklist will vary depending upon the purpose for reading and the type of material.
- In pairs, students are given two minutes to preview the material and jot their responses on the preview form.
- Then the teacher leads the class in developing a strategic plan for reading the material.

Variation:

- When students become proficient in previewing, the teacher may have them develop their own plans for reading the material to present to the class.

Example:

Textbook Preview

Introduction: What is the author talking about?

_____

_____

_____

Headings and Subheads: What are the topics of these sections?

_____

_____

_____

Graphs, charts, maps, and tables: Do I understand how to interpret this information?

_____

_____

_____

Margin notes: What kind of information do they provide?

_____

_____

_____

Summary: Does it provide a clear overview of the chapter?

_____

_____

_____

Questions: Do the questions cover major ideas in the chapter?

_____

_____

_____

Figure 3.11

References

Brown, J. E., Phillips, L., & Stephens, E. C. (1993). *Toward literacy; Theory and applications for teaching writing in the content areas.* Belmont, CA: Wadsworth Publishers, ITP.

Cooney, C. (1994). *Driver's Ed.* New York: Delacorte Press.

Eeds, M., & Cockrum, W. A. (1985). Teaching word meanings by expanding schemata vs. dictionary work vs. reading in context. *Journal of Reading, 28,* 492–497.

Hemmerich, H., Lim, W., & Neel, K. (1994). *Prime time: Strategies for life-long learning in mathematics and science in the middle and high school grades.* Portsmouth, NH: Heinemann.

Ogle, D. (1986). KWL: A teaching model that develops active reading of expository text. *The Reading Teacher, 39,* 564–570.

Richardson, J. S., & Morgan, R. F. (1997). *Reading to learn in the content areas* (3rd edition). Belmont, CA: Wadsworth Publishers, ITP.

CHAPTER 4

Strategies for Constructing

Content literacy strategies for constructing are designed to help students become engaged in content learning. As we discussed in Chapter 2, students must actively process and interact with knowledge and ideas to build meaning. In the last chapter, we presented a number of strategies to help students create an initial connection with content information. In this chapter, we demonstrate how they can build upon that initial connection to integrate and organize new ideas and concepts. Reflective experiences that encourage the development of metacognition are a significant facet of the constructing phase. Students must be able to use their metacognitive knowledge to monitor and adapt their learning strategies.

Scaffolding with Content Literacy

In Chapter 3, we emphasized the strategic nature of learning and the need to provide scaffolding to support student learning. In this chapter, we describe strategies that help students become more engaged in their learning by actively interacting with content. These strategies are designed to be adapted and used in content area classrooms. Frequently teachers use these strategies with print materials; however, many of them also are adaptable to learning from films, videos, and computer software programs. Students' visual literacy can be enhanced greatly through the use of strategies that help them engage in active learning rather than passive viewing. Additionally, many of the strategies in this chapter are applicable for students to use with interactive multimedia on CD-ROMs or with their discoveries on the Internet. Many students spend more time in front of computer screens "surfing the web" than they do with any other type of reading. We cannot assume, however, that students are automatically engaged in constructing meaning at higher levels of understanding during these cyberspace experiences. Through scaffolding, teachers can help students apply constructing strategies in all of their learning experiences, including those on-line.

    In the following profile, highly acclaimed author Jim Murphy shares his insights about writing nonfiction.

An Author's Perspective
Jim Murphy

Jim Murphy was born in New Jersey, and earned a B. A. in English from Rutgers University. Over the years he has worked in a variety of jobs, including a boiler repairperson, chain-link fence installer, and roofer. From 1970 to 1977 he was the managing editor for Clarion Books. He and his wife and two sons now live in Maplewood, New Jersey.

Jim Murphy has written more than twenty-five books and received numerous awards, including the Golden Kite, Orbis Pictus, and Newbery Honor Books.

My main focus as a writer has been non-fiction dealing with the people and events that have shaped America's history. I am particularly drawn to eyewitness accounts that not only let us hear a person's voice, but help us to enter as fully as possible into the events being observed. For me, history is a vibrant story filled with drama, emotion, and complex, intriguing characters.

I grew up in Kearny, New Jersey, a small industrial town that was dominated back then by the sprawling red brick buildings of the Congoleum Nair Company. When I wasn't playing baseball and football, I could be found roaming around town, exploring along the banks of the Passaic River or investigating abandoned factories. I "discovered" books when I was twelve or so, and my parents encouraged me to read as much as I wanted and to pursue some sort of career in books. Their philosophy was that I would always be happier and probably more successful if I did something I truly loved.

I wrote poetry and fiction in high school and college, but I didn't feel confident enough to become a full-time writer after I graduated. Instead, I joined Clarion Books as an editor and stayed there for seven important years. During this time, I worked on picture books, as well as a wide assortment of short and long fiction

and non-fiction, all of which let me get a feel for how a text could be revised, shaped, deepened, played with, and improved. When I was thirty years old, I decided to chance it and left Clarion to become a freelance children's book writer.

I want to create experience books that allow readers to "see" important events in American history through the eyes of people who were actually there and involved. To do this, I take the historical events and shape them into as dramatic a narrative line as possible, using first person quotes, humor, detailed place settings and action (all based on careful research, of course).

Whenever possible I use normal, average people and kids as the focal characters. I do this because the most famous people have already had their stories told many times, so less well-known individuals offer a new, and sometimes more honest perspective. Besides, I think they are easier to relate to and usually their writing is more relaxed and informal (and, thus, easier to enter into).

I have great fun searching out odd, unusual and interesting people and events from our history, and trying to see and feel what life was like for them. I hope my books let readers step into the past in a way that is exciting and entertaining.

Selected Titles

Nonfiction	Fiction
Across America on an Emigrant Train	*The Journal of James Edmond Pease*
A Young Patriot: The American Revolution as Experienced by One Boy	*West to a Land of Plenty: The Diary of Teresa Angelina Viscardi*
Gone A-Whaling: The Lure of the Sea and the Hunt for the Great Whale	
The Boys' War: Confederate and Union Soldiers Talk about the Civil War	
The Great Fire	
The Long Road to Gettysburg	

STRATEGY: Key Questions

Component:	Content Literacy Process:	Organizing for Instruction:
Initiating	Reading	Individual
Constructing	Writing	Pairs
Utilizing	Speaking	Small Group
	Listening	Whole Class
	Viewing	

Description:

Key Questions is a simple strategy designed to help students process the basic elements (Who? What? When? Where? and How?) of what they read. They then display that information on a flipchart, presenting it to a small group or the whole class. This strategy is particular useful with younger readers or with students who have difficulty comprehending at a literal level. Displaying and presenting the information helps students to integrate it into their existing schemata. Key Questions also can be used for short book talks when students are reading different books related to a common theme or topic. This strategy is helpful for teachers, too, as a quick, informal assessment tool.

Procedures:

- The teacher models how to identify the five key questions in a selection: Who? What? When? Where? and How?
- Students then read a designated section of the text or related trade books and record information to answer the five key questions.
- Next they each make a simple flip chart (see Figure 4.1) and portray the information on it.
- Finally they present the information to small groups or the whole class.

Variations:

- Some students are more successful working in pairs as they read and identify the five key questions.
- Some teachers divide the class into five groups and assign each group one of the key questions to answer and display about text material they are all reading.

Example:

Carla Smythe uses Key Questions in her resource room to help students develop a basic understanding of the material in their social studies text. They use their completed flip charts for class presentations and discussion. Then, she has them work in small groups to write newspaper articles based on this information.

Who	What	When	Where	How

Figure 4.1

STRATEGY: Pen-in-Hand

Component:	Content Literacy Process:	Organizing for Instruction:
Initiating	Reading	Individual
Constructing	Writing	Pairs
Utilizing	Speaking	Small Group
	Listening	Whole Class
	Viewing	

Description:

Thomas Devine (1987) uses the term "pen-in-hand" for those functional writing processes (writing without composing) that engage students in interacting with text as they read. We have developed a continuum of these writing-reading interactions (Brown, Phillips, & Stephens, 1993) based on the degree of student involvement (see Figure 4.2). In this strategy, we describe the two most basic pen-in-hand interactions: underlining/highlighting and margin notes. Specific teaching of these interactions is sorely neglected; indeed, in most schools, students are not allowed to write in their textbooks. This practice, however, frequently results in students assuming a passive stance, rapidly skimming through their textbooks without carefully and thoughtfully interacting with the information and ideas. With some adaptations, students can be taught how to use, in an appropriate and effective manner, underlining/highlighting and margin notes as they engage in the constructing of meaning.

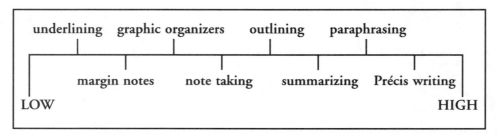

Figure 4.2 Writing-Reading Interactions

Procedures:

- Underlining/highlighting: Teachers model how to interact with text by underlining/highlighting. They provide students with practice by using photocopies of text pages and other selections, consumable materials, and transparencies. Transparencies are placed on text and written on with washable markers.
- Margin Notes: Teachers model how to interact with text by writing notes in the margins. They provide students with practice by using sticky notes that adhere to the text, paper folded lengthwise to serve as a temporary margin, or using any of the items mentioned in underlining/highlighting.

Variations:

- Some teachers find it helpful to provide their students with categories of responses for margin notes, such as reactions, associations, questions, applications, examples, drawings, or symbols.
- Some teachers design margin guides with specific directions for student responses.

Example:

Dave Beatty has students in his math classes use transparency sheets to write margin notes on for each chapter. They make associations, note important information, and ask questions in the notes. Often, he begins class by placing their transparency sheets, one at a time, on the overhead projector and responding to the questions the students have raised.

STRATEGY: X Marks the Spot

Component:	Content Literacy Process:	Organizing for Instruction:
Initiating	Reading	Individual
Constructing	Writing	Pairs
Utilizing	Speaking	Small Group
	Listening	Whole Class
	Viewing	

Description:

With this strategy, students use a symbolic system to help them interact with their reading. It helps to avoid a passive reading of material by providing students with specific things to read for. This three-part reading response code helps them to identify significant information, new information, and information that is unclear.

Procedures:

- The teacher introduces and models the reading response code for students to use when they read independently.
- The code has three parts:

  X means "I've found a key point."

  ! means "I've found some interesting, new information."

  ? means "I'm confused; I have a question about what this means."
- The teacher specifies what students should look for in their reading (e.g., "Mark 4 key points; 2 interesting, new facts; and 3 questions you have.")
- Students use the coding system when they read.
- Their responses are then used as a basis for class discussion.

Variations:

- Some teachers use this strategy in conjunction with margin notes (see p. 70–71 in this chapter for a complete description).

- In some cases, teachers don't prescribe the number of responses students must find in each category, but let them decide as long as they find at least one of each.

- Teachers may create their own adaptation of this coding system to better match their content material and their students' needs.

Examples:

Robyn Greeves discovered that the X Marks the Spot strategy increased her students' active reading of the social studies text. She lists information the students locate from their three categories on charts during class discussion. These charts served as a guide for answering questions and reviewing the major text concepts.

As a math teacher, Alice Linville found that her students often didn't read the explanations in their textbook, but waited for her to explain new concepts and processes in class. She used X Marks the Spot to help direct their reading, adapting it by using only the "X" and "?" codes.

STRATEGY: I wonder why . . .

Component:	Content Literacy Process:	Organizing for Instruction:
Initiating Constructing Utilizing	Reading Writing Speaking Listening Viewing	Individual Pairs Small Group Whole Class

Description:

I wonder why . . . engages students in actively reading text to generate and answer questions. Based on Manzo's (1969) work with ReQuest and Palinscar & Brown's (1984) work with reciprocal teaching, I wonder why . . . provides a format for the teacher to model for students how to construct meaning and monitor their own understanding of new information and ideas.

Procedures:

- The teacher begins by saying, "I wonder why . . ." in reference to something in the text. When first using this strategy, it is better to begin with simple questions such as "I wonder why the author titled this chapter . . ." or "I wonder why the first heading on page 41 states. . . ." As students become more adept, then the questions can become more complex and require higher-level thinking.

- The students engage in silent reading of a set amount of material with the purpose of responding to the teacher's question. Students are provided with note cards or sticky notes to record their responses and pertinent page numbers.

- Initially all responses are accepted and recorded on the board. Then the students and teacher skim through the material again as the teacher models with a think aloud how to answer the question, demonstrating why some responses fit and some don't.

- The procedure is then repeated with the next portion of the text. As the students become familiar with the process, they take turns generating the I wonder why . . . questions and modeling how to respond to the text with a think aloud.

Variation:

- Some teachers find it effective to combine this strategy with data charts (see p. 86–87 in this chapter for a description).

Example:

Dave Holly explains to his science students that what science is really all about is looking for answers to the question *why*. Before he shows films or videos, he gives them 3 or 4 questions to wonder about while viewing. After viewing, they respond to these questions in their content journals (see Chapter 3 for a description).

STRATEGY: VocabMarks

Component:	Content Literacy Process:	Organizing for Instruction:
Initiating	Reading	Individual
Constructing	Writing	Pairs
Utilizing	Speaking	Small Group
	Listening	Whole Class
	Viewing	

Description:

A VocabMark (Brown, Phillips, and Stephens, 1993) is a bookmark made from laminated paper with spaces for students to list unfamiliar words when they encounter them in their reading. There also can be space to write the page number where the word was first encountered so that the student can go back to it easily. This is a quick way for students to make their own vocabulary lists. Students can immediately identify new words while reading and write them on the VocabMark with a water-based pen. In this way, the VocabMark can be reused repeatedly. VocabMarks provide students with an immediate means of interacting with new terms.

Procedures:

- The teacher models finding unfamiliar words while reading and how to record them on a VocabMark. Then VocabMarks are distributed or students make their own.
- On the VocabMarks, students list new words or words that are used in an unfamiliar context.
- They also list the page number where the word was found.
- These new words are transferred to their vocabulary notebooks where students define them and demonstrate how to use them.

Variations:

- Some teachers choose to develop wider VocabMarks so that students can record the word, the page number, and a brief definition when they first encounter it.
- Some teachers structure the use of the VocabMarks by specifying what students must look for (e.g., 2 unfamiliar words; 3 technical terms).

Examples:

James Keith finds that VocabMarks are particularly useful for his students in geometry because they encounter both new words and familiar ones with technical meanings. Students bring their VocabMarks to class on a regular basis for discussion and to share with each other.

Josephine Skolfield has her AP English class use VocabMarks because her students encounter numerous polysyllabic words in their reading. She finds it an effective way for her students to build their vocabularies, because they usually can determine the meaning of new words through context clues. The VocabMarks give students the opportunity to focus on new words.

STRATEGY: Word of the Week

Component:	Content Literacy Process:	Organizing for Instruction:
Initiating	Reading	Individual
Constructing	Writing	Pairs
Utilizing	Speaking	Small Group
	Listening	Whole Class
	Viewing	

Description:

This strategy is designed to encourage students to develop their vocabularies. Each week students select an unfamiliar word whose meaning and use they want to know. They add the word to their vocabulary notebooks. They also use the word regularly during the week, using the word in a sentence on every assignment that they do that week. In addition, each week one class member presents the class word of the week. All class members use the class word as well as their own word in their assignments during the week. This process of making new words their own helps students to construct an ever-widening vocabulary.

Procedures:

- Students identify a new word that they are interested in adding to their vocabularies.
- They list the word, the part of speech, the definitions, and a sentence that provides a context that makes the meaning clear.
- Students use "their word" in all written work for class during that week.
- Students, in turn, have the opportunity to have their word be the class word of the week.
- When students are responsible for the class word of the week, they present the word on Monday by pronouncing it for the class, spelling it, telling the part of speech, giving definitions, and then presenting a sentence that provides a context that makes the meaning clear.

Variations:

- Some teachers have students present the class word of the week without a definition and have the students predict the word's meaning.
- Frequently, teachers find and present their own word of the week to the class.

Examples:

Alfred Martin uses the word of the week strategy in his health class because he wants students to use correct and appropriate terminology.

In Emma McKennon's English language arts classes, students compete to find unusual, yet useful words. She finds that her students continue to use the words in class and in informal discussions with each other. She believes that providing students with opportunities for interacting with the words and presenting them to the class leads to a more sophisticated processing of the language.

STRATEGY: Word Chains

Component:	Content Literacy Process:	Organizing for Instruction:
Initiating	Reading	Individual
Constructing	Writing	Pairs
Utilizing	Speaking	Small Group
	Listening	Whole Class
	Viewing	

Description:

In this strategy, students interact with, make associations, and organize 5–7 new vocabulary words after they have been introduced by the teacher. In most content areas, new vocabulary words are related or connected to other new words or to previously learned words. A word chain provides students with a structure to explore relationship among words, understand how they can be used, and remember their meanings. Seeing connections and relationships generally requires higher-level thinking, so teachers need to model this strategy with the whole class before asking them to do it independently.

Procedures:

- The teacher selects 5–7 new vocabulary words that are related to the same concept and models how to develop a word chain based on their relationships and connections. Frequently, words can be associated to each other in several ways; therefore, more than one word chain can be created using the same words.
- The students, in pairs, are given a group of words. They explore how the words are related or connected to each other. Then they develop a word chain that demonstrates this relationship (see Figure 4.3).
- In pairs, they share their word chains with the rest of the class, explaining the connections.
- Finally, each student writes a short paragraph using the new words in a way that demonstrates their connection.

Variations:

- Some teachers provide students with a longer list of words from which each student or student pair selects a limited number to demonstrate their relationship.

- Some teachers have found this strategy to be a valuable informal assessment tool for determining if students are going beyond literal thinking and developing a deeper conceptual understanding of the content.

Example:

Anna Harris has her sociology class make word chains with terms in their unit on Geriatrics and the Aging Population. Once they have completed their word chains, she has them do a quick write (see Chapter 3, p. 33–34) demonstrating their connection.

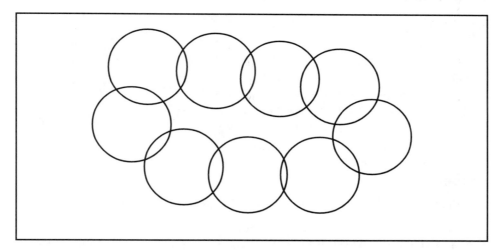

Figure 4.3 Word Chain

STRATEGY: Venn Diagram

(Comparison/Contrast Chart)

Component:	Content Literacy Process:	Organizing for Instruction:
Initiating	Reading	Individual
Constructing	Writing	Pairs
Utilizing	Speaking	Small Group
	Listening	Whole Class
	Viewing	

Description:

A Venn Diagram or comparison/contrast chart is a graphic organizer that uses overlapping circles to present similarities and differences usually between two concepts, ideas, events, objects, or people. The unique characteristics of each are listed in each circle. The shared characteristics are listed in the overlapping area of the circles. Constructing a Venn Diagram requires students to actively interact and think about the information.

Procedures:

- The teacher models developing a Venn Diagram (Figure 4.4) with the whole class.
- Individually or with learning partners, class members list the important characteristics of a concept, idea, object, event, or person in one circle of the diagram.
- Students list the characteristics of the other in the second circle of the diagram.
- Students then use the common overlapping areas of the circles to list similarities.

Variations:

- Teachers may have students list similarities first in the overlapping portion of the circle, and then list the differences second.
- Some teachers, seeking to compare and contrast more than two things, may use three or four circles in their diagrams.

Example:

Harvey Schmidt knew his students would have to write comparison/contrast papers for the state-mandated test in social studies, but this type of writing had always given them trouble. He then taught his students how to use Venn Diagrams to organize their ideas. Next, the students practiced writing comparison/contrast papers using their graphic organizer as a springboard for writing.

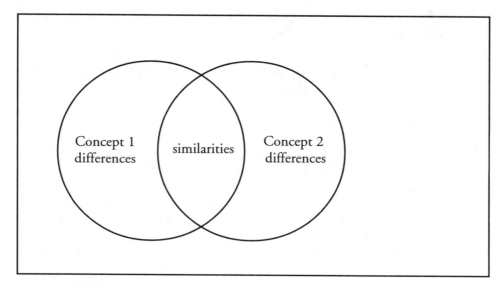

Figure 4.4 Venn Diagram

STRATEGY: Idea Maps

Component:	Content Literacy Process:	Organizing for Instruction:
Initiating	Reading	Individual
Constructing	Writing	Pairs
Utilizing	Speaking	Small Group
	Listening	Whole Class
	Viewing	

Description:

An idea map presents a graphic representation of a specific idea or concept. As with other mapping strategies, it focuses on a central idea and then examines components or ideas related to it. The idea map differs from other mapping strategies in that its central focus is a visual image created as a symbol for the content. Idea maps help students interact with the information and construct meaning. Students organize their thoughts about the central idea and incorporate it into their knowledge base.

Procedures:

- The teacher models an idea map with the whole class. They discuss the various visual images they could select to symbolize the content.
- Students then read a selection and identify the concept or idea to map (or the teacher may have identified it).
- They draw or find a visual that represents or symbolizes the central idea.
- Students create a structure for mapping the related information.
- While working on their idea maps, students will need to refer back to the reading selection to recheck their information or to get more information.
- When idea maps are completed, they can be used for discussion or as a springboard for writing. They can also be displayed in the classroom or put in content notebooks or portfolios.

Variations:

- Teachers vary as to whether they supply a central visual symbol for the idea map or students create their own.

- Some teachers use idea maps as an informal assessment tool by giving students a list of terms related to the topic they've been studying and having them independently create their own idea maps. They also have students write a paragraph describing why they created or selected their particular visual symbol and what the relationship is among the other components.

Examples:

Sandy Carr uses idea mapping in his PE classes to help his students learn about each sport that they are practicing. For example, the following is about baseball.

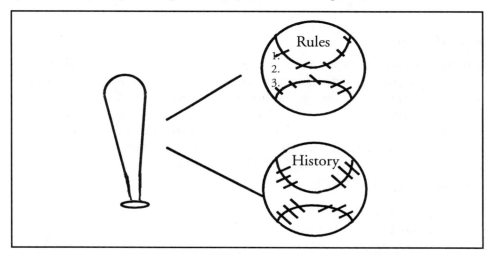

Figure 4.5

As the students in Molly Wesley's English class read *The Great Gatsby*, they used images from it to create ideas and to record key elements of the novel. One student used a mansion, another drew a dock with a light, and another used the following:

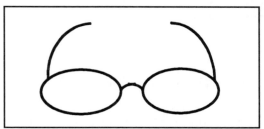

Figure 4.6

STRATEGY: Data Chart

Component:	Content Literacy Process:	Organizing for Instruction:
Initiating	Reading	Individual
Constructing	Writing	Pairs
Utilizing	Speaking	Small Group
	Listening	Whole Class
	Viewing	

Description:

A data chart or matrix (also known as jot chart, grid, question cage, language chart, or semantic features analysis chart) is a versatile, yet simple strategy. It provides students with an organizing structure with which to interact with text as they construct meaning. A data chart serves as an effective note taking device and provides a format for organizing information from several sources. A completed data chart aids students in seeing relationships among major concepts and getting an overall picture of the topic. Johnston and Krueger (1997) also describe its usefulness as a tool for students when they are preparing for state-mandated assessment tests.

Procedures:

- The teacher provides the students with a data chart (see Figure 4.7) and models how to develop it with major categories or student-generated questions using one text.
- Students read the material using the data chart for note taking.
- Students then use their completed data charts as they write follow-up papers or create projects or make presentations.
- Once students become adept at using a data chart to respond to and organize information from one source, the teacher models how to use it for organizing information from several sources (see Figure 4.8).

Variations:

- Some teachers use data charts as listening guides or listening/viewing guides for students.
- Data charts can also provide an effective format for giving speeches.

Examples:

Rocks	Igneous	Sedimentary	Metamorphic
Color			
Shape			
Texture			
Size			

Figure 4.7 Data Chart—Earth Science

Complete this chart after reading the text and two trade books.

	Political Events	Major Figures	Major Battles
What we want to know			
What the text says:			
Trade Book name:			
Trade Book name:			

Figure 4.8 Data Chart–Civil War

Strategy: Text Structure

Component:	Content Literacy Process:	Organizing for Instruction:
Initiating	Reading	Individual
Constructing	Writing	Pairs
Utilizing	Speaking	Small Group
	Listening	Whole Class
	Viewing	

Description:

Text Structure is a basic strategy designed to help students understand the differences between narrative and expository patterns. Understanding these differences is important to the success of students with content area texts. Once students can comfortably differentiate between the two basic types of writing, they should learn how to identify the major expository structures and then how to adjust their reading behavior accordingly (see Expository Text Structure: ROW, p. 90–91).

Procedures:

- The teacher reads to the class short selections that clearly demonstrate the basic differences between fiction and nonfiction.
- With the teacher's guidance, the class develops a checklist (see example) of the characteristics of each type.
- Students, individually, in pairs, or in small groups, find examples of each type and describe their characteristics.

Variations:

- Some teachers use a graphic organizer such as a Venn Diagram to help students compare and contrast the differences between narrative and expository patterns or between specific books.
- Some teachers find that the checklist helps students when writing their own fiction and nonfiction.

Example:

Sample Checklist

Narrative Text	*Expository Text*
Tells a story	Provides information and ideas
Purpose is to entertain or provide aesthetic experience	Purpose is to explain, describe, or persuade
Organized around setting, characters, plot, and theme	Organized around logical relationships between concepts

STRATEGY: Expository Text Structure: ROW

(Read/Organize/Write)

Component:	Content Literacy Process:	Organizing for Instruction:
Initiating	Reading	Individual
Constructing	Writing	Pairs
Utilizing	Speaking	Small Group
	Listening	Whole Class
	Viewing	

Description:

Expository Text Structure: ROW focuses on helping students understand different kinds of expository patterns. Built upon a basic understanding of the major differences between narrative and expository texts, this strategy provides students with the following acronym for working with six common expository patterns.

Read

Organize

Write

The patterns are sequence/directions; listing/description; definition/explanation; comparison/contrast; problem/solution; and cause/effect. They should be taught one at a time, beginning with the ones that are most commonly found in the reading material used in that content class.

Procedures:

- The teacher presents an expository text pattern using short, clear examples for the class to read.
- With teacher guidance, the class develops a working definition of the pattern (see example) and a graphic organizer that represents it.
- Based on current content topics, the students write a selection using the text pattern they are learning.
- Then the ROW (Read/Organize/Write) process is repeated with another expository text pattern until the class has learned all of the patterns.

Variations:

- Some teachers have students find examples of expository text patterns in other materials that they read outside of class.
- Some teachers vary slightly the names of the expository text patterns to more closely fit the patterns found in their particular content material. For example, "definition/explanation" might be termed "explanation/process" or "sequence/directions" might be separated into two distinct patterns.

Examples:

Sequence/Directions: reflects passing of time or steps to be followed

Listing/Description: describes or defines using details or examples

Definition/Explanation: defines or explains a process, how something works or is done

Comparison/Contrast: focuses on similarities and differences

Problem/Solution: presents a problem and a solution to the problem

Cause/Effect: presents a cause and then at least one effect or result

STRATEGY: Cubing

Component:	Content Literacy Process:	Organizing for Instruction:
Initiating	Reading	Individual
Constructing	Writing	Pairs
Utilizing	Speaking	Small Group
	Listening	Whole Class
	Viewing	

Description:

Cubing, developed by Cowen and Cowen (1980), provides the opportunity for students to construct meaning about a specific topic from six different perspectives. Each side of the cube (see Figure 4.9) has the students use different thinking processes:

Description (What is it like?)

Comparison (What is it similar to or different from?)

Association (What does it make you think of?)

Analysis (How is it made or what is it composed of?)

Application (What can you do with it? How is it used?)

Argumentation (Take a stand, arguing for or against it.)

Procedures:

- The teacher models cubing with the class.
- Students select a topic for writing.
- Students write for three to five minutes on each of the six sides of the cube:
  describe it
  compare it
  associate it
  analyze it
  apply it
  argue for or against it
- Students use their completed cubes as the springboard for longer writing assignments or for class discussion.

Variations:

- Some teachers adapt the designations on each of the six sides to make them more appropriate to specific content areas.
- Students may work in small groups with each member writing about a different side of the cube and then combing their work.

Example:

Alisa Chaney has her students review their study of the Civil War by selecting a topic about it. Each student completes a cube. Once the students have completed their cubes, they attach yarn to them and tie them to hangers to make classroom mobiles.

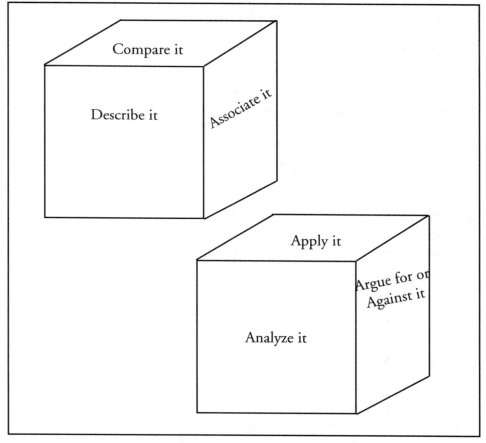

Figure 4.9

STRATEGY: Learning Partner Journal

Component:	Content Literacy Process:	Organizing for Instruction:
Initiating	Reading	Individual
Constructing	Writing	Pairs
Utilizing	Speaking	Small Group
	Listening	Whole Class
	Viewing	

Description:

The learning partner journal is designed to provide students with a forum to communicate with their learning partner in a systematic way. This type of journal can be used in a number of ways (reading reactions, raising questions, dialogues about concepts, tips on doing problems, among others) to establish a working/learning relationship between two classmates.

Procedures:

- The teacher determines how learning partners will be assigned.
- The teacher models responding to a learning partner.
- Students practice responding in their journals.
- The two-way communication begins by sharing journal entries.
- Students periodically meet with the teacher for feedback sessions.
- At the end of a specified period, the learning partners reflect on their experience.

Variations:

- Some teachers find that the journal writing experience is strengthened if learning partners remain together for at least a marking period.
- Others have their students remain with the same learning partner for the duration of a unit or topic.
- In some classes, the learning partners are a triad, with three students involved.

Examples:

Paul Phillips' science class students used their learning partner journals to share observations and reactions during their unit on the environment.

In Monique Cormier's French class, the learning partner journal is literally a dialogue between students as they practice new vocabulary and syntax. She begins class by having students respond to either a question or a comment in their journals. They then exchange journals and respond to what each other has written, returning them for another exchange.

STRATEGY: Brainwriting

Component:	Content Literacy Process:	Organizing for Instruction:
Initiating	Reading	Individual
Constructing	Writing	Pairs
Utilizing	Speaking	Small Group
	Listening	Whole Class
	Viewing	

Description:

Brainwriting (Brown, Phillips, & Stephens, 1993) is a strategy designed to help students interact with material they are reading by generating ideas based on it. This interacting with ideas helps students to clarify and develop the meanings they are constructing from their reading. It also fosters metacognition, as students must re-check and verify their information.

Procedures:

- The teacher identifies a topic for student writing.
- The class is divided into small groups of between three to five students.
- Individually, each student writes several ideas that they remember from their reading on the topic.
- After approximately 5 minutes of writing, students put their papers in the middle of the group.
- Each group member takes another paper, reads what was written, and adds to it.
- They repeat the process until they have read and added to all of the papers.
- During this process, students may question each other about what they wrote; they also may need to return to the original text to check or clarify information.
- Each group develops a master list to share with the rest of the class.
- The master list can be modified as the class and teacher determine what is appropriate.

Variations:

- Some teachers have students do this process with a learning partner rather than in a small groups.
- Some teachers have students develop writing assignments from one or more of the ideas.
- Some teachers have students select between five to seven of the ideas that are related and use them as the basis for an essay.

Example:

In Jacob Henry's economics class, ideas are shared through brainwriting when students work cooperatively to deepen their understanding of major concepts from their readings. Mr. Henry finds that difficult concepts are readily made more accessible through the interaction of students building on each other's ideas. As a follow-up to brainwriting, students take ideas from the master list to generate topics for their major papers.

STRATEGY: Pass It On

Component:	Content Literacy Process:	Organizing for Instruction:
Initiating	Reading	Individual
Constructing	Writing	Pairs
Utilizing	Speaking	Small Group
	Listening	Whole Class
	Viewing	

Description:

Pass It On is a group writing strategy to help students work together to build continuity and fluency in their writing. In small groups, they develop a collective rough draft. This strategy provides students with opportunities for creative interaction with concepts and ideas from any content area.

Procedures:

- The teacher begins by creating and reading a brief outline of a possible scenario based on a current topic the class is studying.
- The teacher poses speculative questions to the class based on the scenario.
- The class then divides into groups of three to develop the outline into a complete scenario.
- The group members alternate writing for five minutes, each building on the previous writing.
- Next the group members review and revise their scenario.
- Each group reads its scenario to the whole class.
- These drafts may be used as a springboard for more polished written work.

Variation:

- Some teachers modify this process so that each member of the small group is writing simultaneously.

Example:

William Forrest, a science teacher, concluded a unit on the Rain Forest using the Pass It On Strategy. He began with a brief outline of a scenario of an expedition to the Amazon. He posed several hypothetical questions to the class. In this writing, he wanted his students to relate to the natural environment and reflect the principles they had studied.

STRATEGY: Scintillating Sentences and Quizzical Quotes

Component:	Content Literacy Process:	Organizing for Instruction:
Initiating	Reading	Individual
Constructing	Writing	Pairs
Utilizing	Speaking	Small Group
	Listening	Whole Class
	Viewing	

Description:

Scintillating Sentences and Quizzical Quotes is a strategy adapted from sentence collecting (Speaker & Speaker, 1991). It engages students in reading for information and helps them develop higher-level thinking skills such as analysis and evaluation. This strategy involves students in their reading and helps them to make connections between what they read and their own lives.

Procedures:

- The teacher directs the students to find a sentence from their reading to share with the class. The teacher either specifies what the students should look for in a sentence or tells them to find any sentence that they want to share. A Scintillating Sentence usually is one that the student thinks represents a significant idea, illustrates a particular point of view, or has special meaning for understanding the content. A Quizzical Quote is a sentence that the student doesn't understand or thinks that others in the class may find confusing.

- Once students have selected their sentences, they write them on sentence strips or chart paper to display around the room. Each sentence is recorded with the author, title, page number, and the student's initials.

- Students walk around the room and read each other's sentences.

- Then the sentences become the focal point for class discussion. One by one, students read their sentences and explain why they selected them. If the sentence is a Quizzical Quote, they ask others in the class to explain what the sentence means.

Variations:

- An effective variation puts more emphasis on having students respond to each other's sentence. This is accomplished by putting chart paper next to each sentence strip displayed around the room. As students read each other's sentences, they write their comments about the sentence on the chart paper.

- Some teachers use the sentences as a springboard for writing. Students either write about their own sentence or select one that is displayed to write about.

Examples:

Diane Horst uses Scintillating Sentences and Quizzical Quotes in her German class. She finds that it helps the students focus on understanding what they are reading. It also provides them with practice in using the language orally, as they must explain in German to the class why they selected a particular sentence or else ask the other students to explain what they think it means.

Randy Powell uses Quizzical Quotes to get his social studies class to ask questions about what they read. Because they won't admit they don't understand something, he has them select a sentence, several sentences, or a paragraph that they think will be confusing to the rest of the class. Each student then has the opportunity to quiz the rest of the class until meaning has been developed.

STRATEGY: Paired Guided Reading

Component:	Content Literacy Process:	Organizing for Instruction:
Initiating	Reading	Individual
Constructing	Writing	Pairs
Utilizing	Speaking	Small Group
	Listening	Whole Class
	Viewing	

Description:

Paired Guided Reading, based on Manzo's guided-reading procedure (1975), is a structured process for engaging pairs of students in constructing meaning with content material. It provides a format for students to interact with text in multiple ways and to verbalize and share with another reader. "Constructing meaning during reading means going back and forth between reading relatively small segments of text and discussing the ideas encountered" (Beck et al., 1997, p. 20). Paired Guided Reading is particularly useful with complex or technical text and for students who have difficulty monitoring their own understanding of text. It also helps to develop metacognition as students check and re-check their understanding of their reading.

Procedures:

- The teacher introduces a reading selection to the class using a short, initiating strategy and then tells the students they will be reading and discussing it in segments with their learning partner.

- The teacher directs the students to read a set amount of text and establishes a specific purpose (e.g. Read the first four paragraphs to find three major causes of pollution.). Students are told to turn their books over when they are finished reading and record on separate note cards or sticky notes what they remember.

- Student pairs then compare and discuss their notes, grouping the notes that are similar. They monitor themselves by asking: "Did we leave out any important information? Was there anything we didn't understand? Did we mix-up anything?" Next the student pairs turn over their books to reread the material as they check, add to, or change their notes.

- If more material is to be read, then the previous steps are repeated. Finally, the student pairs organize their notes into a graphic organizer that demonstrates the relationships of the ideas.

Variation:

- Frequently teachers have students return at another time to the graphic organizer they created to review their notes and then write a summary of the information.

Example:

Melinda Mathews was concerned that her students were either unable or unwilling to read the science text. Finally, she tried Paired Guided Reading, and for the first time, students were engaged with the text.

STRATEGY: Missing Words

Component:	Content Literacy Process:	Organizing for Instruction:
Initiating	Reading	Individual
Constructing	Writing	Pairs
Utilizing	Speaking	Small Group
	Listening	Whole Class
	Viewing	

Description:

Missing Words, an adaptation of the cloze procedure (Taylor, 1953), engages students in reading a selection with certain words deleted, and then predicting in writing the missing words. This is followed by a whole class or small group discussion during which students discuss their word choices and use think-aloud procedures to model their thought processes. The Missing Words strategy helps students learn to draw upon their prior knowledge, use their metacognitive skills, think inferentially, and understand relationships among ideas as they construct the text. Teachers can also use Missing Words as an informal assessment tool.

Procedures:

- The teacher selects a passage that students haven't read and deletes certain words, leaving the beginning and ending sentences intact. The words to be deleted depend upon the teacher's instructional goals. They may be key vocabulary words; certain parts of speech; deletions based on a numerical pattern such as every 7th or 10 word; or specific words selected by the teacher.

- The teacher also prepares a short, relatively easy passage to demonstrate to the class how to use the Missing Words strategy. First, the teacher models how to skim the entire passage to get an overview of it. Next, the teacher demonstrates how to read the material, looking for clues to help predict the missing words. Then, using a think-aloud, the teacher models the metacognitive process of rereading the passage, monitoring the word choices and their effect upon the meaning of the entire passage. Finally, the teacher compares the completed passage with the original and evaluates the word choices.

- The students, individually or in pairs, use the Missing Words strategy on a passage. Then, in small groups or as the entire class, they discuss their word choices and practice using think-alouds. Finally, they read the passage as it was originally written.

Variations:

- Most teachers have found that it is detrimental to grade the students' completed Missing Words passages. (Some simply give credit or no credit.) Learning to use the Missing Words strategy can improve students' reading, but it is a complex thinking task that requires risk-taking in a non-threatening environment.

- Many teachers have found Missing Words to be most successful when the emphasis is upon the students describing and analyzing their thinking processes rather than upon comparing the completed passage with the original one.

Example:

Donald Jackson used the Missing Words strategy with a passage from The Cornerstones of Freedom series, *The Roaring Twenties*, by R. Conrad Stein (1994, pp. 8–9) with his history class.

The single device that produced the decade's most revolutionary change was the automobile. A generation earlier, _____ were playthings for the rich. But _____ production drove the prices _____, and by the 1920's, anyone with a decent job could aspire to own a "gas buggy."

American families viewed them as four-wheeled dreams. When a farm housewife was asked why she chose to buy a _____ even though the family did not own a bathtub, she answered, "Because you can't drive to town in a _____."

By 1929, 23 million cars jammed American _____, triple the number of nine years earlier. Almost half a million Americans _____ in auto manufacturing plants. King of the industry was the _____ Motor Company of Detroit. In 1908, Henry Ford had introduced a simple, reliable _____ he called the Model T. It had a twenty-horsepower engine, which gave it a top _____ of forty miles per hour. Early models cost $850.

STRATEGY: QAR

Component:	Content Literacy Process:	Organizing for Instruction:
Initiating	Reading	Individual
Constructing	Writing	Pairs
Utilizing	Speaking	Small Group
	Listening	Whole Class
	Viewing	

Description:

QAR, the question/answer relationship (Raphael, 1984, 1986), helps students to understand different levels of questions and the relationships between questions and their answers. Too many students respond to questions either with a literal answer or by declaring that "it" isn't in the book and therefore they can't answer it. QAR presents four levels of questions/answer relationships: Right There; Think and Search; You and the Author; and On Your Own (see example). It also provides students with another way to understand their thinking processes and develop their metacognitve abilities.

Procedures:

- The teacher introduces QAR using a visual aid and a short selection to demonstrate the relationships.
- The teacher models identifying and answering questions at each level of QAR.
- With teacher guidance, students practice identifying and answering questions at each of the levels.
- Students then apply QAR to the reading of their regular texts.

Variations:

- With younger students or readers who experience difficulty, teachers may want to introduce and practice one level at a time before introducing the next level.
- Some teachers find that these three levels of question/answer relationships are less confusing for students than four: Right There; Think and Search; Author and Me.
- An adaptation provided by Vacca and Vacca (1996) identifies two broad categories of information: In the Text and In My Head. Students are helped to see that Right There and Think and Search fall under the In the Text category, while On My Own and Author and You come under In My Head.

Example:

Where is the answer?

(1) Right there! (The answer is found in the text. The words in the question can usually be found in the same sentence with the answer.)

(2) Think and search! (The answer is in the text, but the words are probably not in the same sentence. You must read the text, look for ideas that you can put together, and think about what the author is saying.)

(3) You and the author! (The author of the text gave you some ideas and made you think, but you must figure out what you know and use it to answer the question.)

(4) On Your Own! (You must apply what you know and what you have learned to answer the question.)

STRATEGY: Concept Collection

Component:	Content Literacy Process:	Organizing for Instruction:
Initiating	Reading	Individual
Constructing	Writing	Pairs
Utilizing	Speaking	Small Group
	Listening	Whole Class
	Viewing	

Description:

Concept collection (Brown, Phillips, & Stephens, 1993) engages students in higher-level thinking by having them take an active role in constructing concepts. Concept collecting engages students in identifying concepts and the evidence that supports them. The format engages students in assessing their prior knowledge, then finding evidence to confirm or reject, and finally adding new concepts to their understanding of the topic. A value of this strategy is that it helps students build conceptual learning rather than just factual knowledge. Developing concepts as opposed to listing facts requires teacher modeling and a substantial amount of guided practice over a period of time. Every step of this procedure will initially require teacher assistance and class discussion.

Procedures:

- The teacher has the students divide their paper into four columns and label them: Familiar Concepts, Evidence, New Concepts, Evidence.
- Before students read the selection, they fill out the first column by listing major concepts that they already understand about the topic.
- Next, they read the selection, article, or chapter. As they read, they record any evidence that supports what they already know about the major concepts.
- After completing the selection, students identify and list what they consider to be new concepts they've developed as a result of reading.
- They then record evidence supporting these new concepts.
- The class, through discussion, develops a master list of concepts learned about the topic from the selection. This requires that they engage in rereading and checking portions of the selection for accuracy.

Variation:

- Some teachers label the second column, Factual Evidence, to help students see how concepts must be supported by facts.

Example:

To help students understand the difference between concepts and facts or evidence, Wesley Mayes uses the following example in his unit on statistics.

Concept   Attending sporting events is a major pastime in our community.

Evidence   The local newspaper reported that for the past five years attendance at local high school football and basketball games increased by 30%.

STRATEGY: Opinion Guide

Component:	Content Literacy Process:	Organizing for Instruction:
Initiating	Reading	Individual
Constructing	Writing	Pairs
Utilizing	Speaking	Small Group
	Listening	Whole Class
	Viewing	

Description:

Opinion Guides provide students with a series of statements to respond to from two different perspectives, their own and that of the author's. Using Opinion Guides, students cannot approach their reading from the standpoint of merely "extracting information"; nor can they think only in terms of their own reactions and opinions. Opinion Guides engage students in higher-level thinking as they actively read both to construct their own understanding of the text and also to understand the author's position. When students compare their opinions with those of the author, they also engage in reflective thinking.

Procedures:

- The teacher creates an opinion guide by writing a series of statements, usually 3 to 7, from material the students will be reading. The statements should require students to think beyond a literal level of comprehension. Each statement is preceded by two columns, one labeled "You" and the other, "Author" (see Figure 4.10).
- The students read the opinion guide and mark whether they agree or disagree with each statement prior to reading the text.
- While they read the text, the students actively search for ideas that will help them understand the author's opinions.
- After reading the selection, the students mark what they think the author's opinion is for each statement on the opinion guide. They must cite evidence from the text to support their positions.
- Students may also go back to their original positions and modify them.
- Then in small groups or as the whole class, students discuss each statement, comparing their opinions with each other and with the author's opinions. They also must reach consensus on whether they think the author's opinions are based on ideas from the text.

- Finally, each student writes a persuasive paper either in support of or in opposition to the author's position. They must document the evidence from which they draw their conclusions.

Variation:

- Because the processes involved in the Opinion Guide require some fairly sophisticated thinking skills, some teachers initially work with portions of it until the students gain the skills to do all of it.

Example:

Tom Valdez created an Opinion Guide for the students in his government class to use when they read campaign literature from the various candidates for state office.

YOU agree/disagree		AUTHOR agree/disagree		
❑	❑	❑	❑	The government should give money to parents to send their children to any public, private, or religious school they choose.
❑	❑	❑	❑	Taxes should be eliminated as a means of financing schools.
❑	❑	❑	❑	Letting parents choose what schools they send their children to would result in greater racial harmony.
❑	❑	❑	❑	The public schools have succeeded as a melting pot in bringing together diverse racial, cultural, and economic groups.
❑	❑	❑	❑	Competition will improve the public schools.

Figure 4.10

STRATEGY: Beyond SQ3R

Component:	Content Literacy Process:	Organizing for Instruction:
Initiating	Reading	Individual
Constructing	Writing	Pairs
Utilizing	Speaking	Small Group
	Listening	Whole Class
	Viewing	

Description:

SQ3R is a time-honored study system, but increasingly teachers find that helping their classes create their own systems based on sound instructional principles and tailored to specific content areas is more successful. Designing a study system helps students develop a stronger awareness and understanding of their own metacognitive abilities, that is, how they learn. Students also display more willingness to practice and use a study system they have helped to create.

Procedures:

- The teacher begins by displaying several study systems and having the class analyze what they all have in common. Some examples include:

SQ3R (Robinson, 1961)
- S: Survey
- Q: Question
- 3R: Read, Recite, Review

PORPE (Simpson et al., 1988)
- P: Predict
- O: Organize
- R: Rehearse
- P: Practice
- E: Evaluate

STAR (Brown, Phillips, & Stephens, 1993)
- S: Skim & set purpose
- T: Think
- A: Anticipate & adjust
- R: Review & retell

- Next the students discuss what they do when they read and study text materials in this content area. Then they make two lists, one labeled "Successful," the other, "Unsuccessful."
- Then in small groups, the students develop study systems specifically for this content area and create acronyms for them.
- The study systems are presented by each group to the entire class. After demonstration and discussion, the class selects one to use.

Variations:

- Some teachers have the class select 2 or 3 study systems to use, thus allowing for learning differences.
- Some teachers have the students try all of the study systems for awhile, and then lead the class in evaluating and revising them, sometimes combining elements of several to create the final class study system.

Examples:

GOAL
- G: Glance through
- O: Order thoughts
- A: Adjust
- L: Learn by retelling

LAFF
- L: Look over material
- A: Ask questions to be answered
- F: Find answers by reading
- F: Follow through by reflecting & reviewing

STRATEGY: Process Logs

Component:	Content Literacy Process:	Organizing for Instruction:
Initiating	Reading	Individual
Constructing	Writing	Pairs
Utilizing	Speaking	Small Group
	Listening	Whole Class
	Viewing	

Description:

Process logs are designed to help students think about learning. The process log provides students with opportunities to reflect on their learning and develop their metacognitive abilities. These logs can be used in two primary ways: first, students can reflect on prompts dealing with content; or second, they can respond to prompts about *how* they learn content.

Procedures:

- The teacher models how to respond to process prompts.
- The students practice responding to sample prompts.
- The teacher prepares a prompt for students.
- Students respond to the prompt.

Variation:

- In some cases, students develop their own prompts and respond to them.

Example:

The following are sample prompts for both content and metacognitive awareness.

Content:

Explain the new information (ideas, concepts, etc.) in your own words.

Explain how the new information fits in with something you already know.

How does the new information cause you to change your mind about something you thought you knew?

Explain the new concept to a friend, to a younger student, or to a relative.

Describe how you can use what you've learned.

Explain why it was important to learn this information.

Self-Awareness and Metacognition:

Describe yourself as a science student (or math or any other content area).

Describe yourself as 5th grader (or any other grade level).

Describe what you do when you read something that is difficult.

Explain how you did this assignment.

Explain how you figured out the answer to this problem (this question).

Describe what didn't make sense to you in this assignment (or problem or question).

Explain what you do when you're having trouble with an assignment (or problem or question).

Describe what you've accomplished during this class period (or day or week).

Describe how you prepared for this test.

Explain why your work wasn't done on time.

Write about one problem in last night's assignment that was hard for you.

STRATEGY: Focus Sentences

Component:	Content Literacy Process:	Organizing for Instruction:
Initiating	Reading	Individual
Constructing	Writing	Pairs
Utilizing	Speaking	Small Group
	Listening	Whole Class
	Viewing	

Description:

Focus Sentences is a strategy to give students guidance and experience improving their own writing. Writing is a significant way for students to construct meaning. Helping students to revise and edit their writing helps them to develop deeper levels of understanding, better focus, and more clarity. In preparation for this strategy, the teacher begins by selecting sentences from student papers that demonstrate representative problems for the class or are examples of strong, clear writing. The sentences that the teacher selects should be used anonymously; under *no* circumstances should students ever be identified in this process. The teacher, in a mini-lesson, works with the class to recognize the problems and to see how to revise them for clarity and meaning or to analyze what makes effective writing. The teacher focuses on typical problems that often appear in students' writing and also works with specific skills they need to develop.

Procedures:

- The teacher writes 3–5 sentences on the board or on an overhead projector and helps the class analyze what makes them strong and what needs to be improved.
- Students are then given sentences to revise either individually or in pairs.
- Students then share their revised sentences with the whole class.
- The teacher and class members discuss the edited sentences, emphasizing clarity of meaning.
- Students then engage in writing that will provide them with an opportunity to apply what they have been learning with Focus Sentences.

Variations:

- Some teachers are uncomfortable using writing examples from current students. Instead they collect examples from previous students they have had in class.
- Other teachers like to use examples from professional writing in their content areas.

Example:

Randy Beck's students write extensively in his science classes. Among the various types of writing they do are lab and demonstration reports; they also write and publish a science newsletter. Mr. Beck uses Focus Sentences to help his students learn to write about science in a way that will clearly communicate their ideas to others.

STRATEGY: Note Taking: Do It Yourself!

Component:	Content Literacy Process:	Organizing for Instruction:
Initiating	Reading	Individual
Constructing	Writing	Pairs
Utilizing	Speaking	Small Group
	Listening	Whole Class
	Viewing	

Description:

Effective note taking is one of the most important skills that students can develop. Yet, too often its development is left to chance or receives minimal attention. The actual recording of notes is only part of the process—the real value lies in returning to the notes: reacting, adding, organizing, and using them in some way. These actions are what lead to a deeper construction of meaning and the eventual integration into one's schema. While there are numerous available note taking systems, what seems to be important is to help students develop a system that works for them within the context of a specific content area and can be adapted to verbal and visual presentations as well as printed materials.

Procedures:

- The teacher prepares a short verbal or visual presentation or a reading selection to use for modeling note taking. Next the teacher selects an appropriate note taking system and, based upon it, prepares a note taking guide that is partially completed.

- Together the teacher and students complete the note taking guide. As they work on it, the teacher helps the students to develop their own shorthand system and abbreviations for frequently used words.

- Next the teacher provides practice in using the other components of the note taking system, so that students understand that a note taking system is more than just recording notes.

- Finally, the teacher provides utilizing experiences wherein the students must actually use their notes to complete a project, solve a problem, or write for publication (see Chapter 5 for examples).

Variations:

- Some teachers begin teaching simple note taking skills by providing students with the headings: who, what, when, where, why, and how, followed by a respond prompt such as "What this means to me."
- Many teachers find that note taking is greatly enhanced by adding graphic organizers such as mapping, Venn Diagrams, and data charts (see description on p. 82–87).

Examples:

R3 (adapted from Brown, Phillips, & Stephens, 1993)

A 3-step approach using two notebook pages (see Figure 4.11):
1. Record the notes.
2. Respond to the notes with questions and answers.
3. React to what you are learning and make associations that will help you understand and remember the material.

Verbatim Split Page Procedure (VSPP) (Readance, Bean, & Baldwin, 1998, p. 210)
1. Record notes on left hand side of paper split into a 2-column format (40% on left, 60% on right).
2. Reorganize, interpret, and expand upon the notes using the right hand column.
3. Use the notes for studying.

Notes	Questions and Answers	Reactions:
		Make associations to learn new material:

Figure 4.11 Two notebook pages facing one another

References

Beck, I. L., McKeown, M. G., Hamilton, R. L., & Kucan, L. (1997). *Questioning the author: An approach for enhancing student engagement with text.* Newark, DE: International Reading Association.

Brown, J. E., & Stephens, E. C. (1995). *Teaching young adult literature: Sharing the connection.* Belmont, CA: Wadsworth Publishers, ITP.

Brown, J. E., Phillips, L., & Stephens, L. (1993). *Toward Literacy; Theory and applications for teaching writing in the content areas.* Belmont, CA: Wadsworth Publishers, ITP.

Cowen, G., & Cowen, E. (1980). *Writing.* New York: Wiley.

Devine, T. (1987). *Teaching study skills: A guide for teachers* (2nd edition). Newton, MA: Allyn & Bacon.

Johnston, M., & Krueger, M. (Summer 1997). Using a matrix to organize and respond to text. *Michigan Reading Journal, 30,* 3, 30–38.

Manzo, A. V. (1975). The guided reading procedure. *Journal of Reading, 18,* 287–291.

Manzo, A. V. (1969). The request procedure. *Journal of Reading, 11,* 123–126.

Palinscar, A. S., & Brown, A. L. (1984). Reciprocal teaching of comprehension-fostering and comprehension-monitoring activities. *Cognition and Instruction, 1,* 117–175.

Raphael, T. (1984). Teaching learners about sources of information for answering comprehension questions. *Journal of Reading, 27,* 303–311.

Raphael, T. (1986). Teaching questions/answer relationships, revisited. *The Reading Teacher, 39,* 516–522.

Readance, J. E., Bean, T. W., & Baldwin, R. S. (1998). *Content area literacy: An integrated approach.* (3rd edition). Dubuque, IA: Kendall/Hunt.

Robinson, F. P. (1961). *Effective study* (revised edition). New York: Harper & Row.

Simpson, M. L., Hayes, C. G., Stahl, N., Connor, R. T., & Weaver, D. (1988). An initial validation of a study strategy system. *Journal of reading behavior, 20,* 149–180.

Speaker, R. B., Jr. & Speaker, P. (1991). Sentence collecting: Authentic literacy events in the classroom. *Journal of Reading, 5* (2), 92–95.

Stein, R. C. (1994). *The Roaring Twenties.* Chicago, IL: Childrens Press.

Taylor, W. (1953). Cloze procedure: A new tool for measuring readability. *Journalism Quarterly, 30,* 415–433.

Vacca, R. T., & Vacca, J. A. (1996). *Content area reading* (5th edition). New York: HarperCollins.

CHAPTER 5

Strategies for Utilizing

Utilizing is the bridge between the classroom and the real world. It is the place in the instructional framework where teachers provide students with opportunities to act upon or apply what they are learning. While there has been ongoing discussion of relevance in the curriculum, too often in the classroom it is neglected or consists of a cursory description of how what the students are learning will help them "someday."

For today's students, the traditional "read the chapter, take an exam" approach to learning is not only irrelevant, but also tedious. Many students are not motivated by grades; they need to see that there is an immediate purpose to their learning and that it will have meaning beyond the classroom walls. When students have opportunities to utilize what they are learning, these experiences have a longer-lasting impact on them.

Often when students ask "Why do we have to do this?" they actually mean, "How does this connect to my life?" Television, computers, and the Internet have erased many artificial social and geographical boundaries in the world; now is the time for the curriculum to include the world beyond the schoolhouse door. Educating today's youth means helping them to use the knowledge and skills that they are learning to solve problems, to create new ideas, and to think about things in different ways.

In Chapter 2, we described utilizing as the component of the instructional framework where students become more independent, where they gain an ever-increasing power to act upon the meanings that they have constructed. In a real sense, the component of utilizing might be considered an independent thinking/action component because students must exercise significant mental bridging. Thinking people make informed choices, form considered judgments, solve problems, debate alternatives rationally, apply learning, recognize relationships, and generalize learning from one situation to another. These abilities allow students to look beyond the classroom to their communities and the world.

Scaffolding with Content Literacy

In the instructional framework, the component of utilizing is, in keeping with the road map analogy, the ultimate destination. When students arrive at this phase, they have already experienced the initiating and constructing phases. They are now at the point where they can gain assurance to be in command of their own learning. In utilizing, students are becoming ever more independent as learners. The scaffolding that supported students through the first two components of the instructional framework is reduced in this phase. As students use strategies designed to help them construct new meanings, they are becoming ever more independent in their learning. Scaffolding is a support system to help students to learn to use strategies to become increasingly independent, taking responsibility for their learning. The strategies in this chapter help students to take the initiative to learn beyond the classroom.

The Two Facets of Utilizing

In Chapters 3 and 4, we described content literacy strategies to improve student learning through the components of initiating and constructing. We have divided this chapter on utilizing into two major sections. Utilizing is about those *experiences and activities* that provide students with opportunities to use and demonstrate their learning. But it is also about the *content literacy processes and strategies* that make these experiences and activities meaningful. For example, a simulation in a health class might be the culminating experience of a unit on infectious diseases. The purpose and value of the learning experience can be lost without careful, thoughtful planning of both the simulation and the strategies that prepare and support students to participate in it in a meaningful way. A lab in science on different sources of microorganisms in water may be a significant utilizing experience, but students also need to be able to record their observations in their lab manuals and then report their findings in a manner that is consistent with what scientists actually do. A group project in social studies to recreate how early settlers lived and worked in their community may be a valuable utilizing activity, but with the structure of a planning guide, project journal, and discussion continuum students also develop important content literacy strategies. In other words, in order for learning in most content classrooms to go beyond the constructing phase, teachers must design appropriate experiences and activities and then have students involved in content literacy strategies that contribute to their ability to utilize their learning.

To accommodate the two facets of utilizing, the structure of this chapter departs slightly from the format established in Chapters 3 and 4. It is divided into two sections: Section I describes a number of generic experiences and activities that teachers may adapt to many different content areas for the utilizing component of the instructional framework; Section II describes content literacy strategies to help structure and support these learning experiences and activities. This chapter also includes perspectives from two highly regarded authors: Dorothy Hinshaw Patent and Janet Bode. In the first of these, noted author, Dorothy Hinshaw Patent, whose books about wildlife and the natural environment have received numerous awards, gives us her insights.

An Author's Perspective
DOROTHY HINSHAW PATENT

Dorothy Hinshaw Patent was born in Rochester, Minnesota, but her family moved to the San Francisco Bay Area when she was nine years old. From the time she was very young, she loved animals and nature. She earned a bachelor's degree in Biological Sciences from Stanford University and an M.A. and Ph.D. in Zoology from the University of California, Berkeley. She and her husband have two grown sons and now live in Missoula, Montana.

Dorothy Hinshaw Patent has received numerous awards, including the Golden Kite Award, the Eva Gordon Award from the American Nature Study Society, and the Library of Congress Children's Book of the Year.

As a child I was always interested in nature and had snakes, fish, and frogs as pets, instead of playing with dolls. I was lucky to be born into a family that encouraged my interest in nature so I was able to follow my heart. Even if family and friends aren't understanding and supportive, however, it is important for us not to lose sight of the things that matter most to us as individuals and to pursue our passions.

I began writing in 1972 and have published more than 100 books. I do my best to have personal experiences with the subjects I write about and therefore travel a lot, often to other countries. I hope my writing does more than present the facts about the natural world and about our human history. I want my readers to feel their connection to other living things and to the continuity of the generations of humans through time. At the same time, I hope they will appreciate and respect the differences between them and other species and see that each has its rightful place on our small planet. I want children and young people to learn about the many

ways there have been and are to be human and to appreciate how much easier life is today than it was even for their own grandparents and great grandparents. Again, I see the importance of respect for differences here, as well as celebrating human creativity through the ages.

Nonfiction books make a great starting place for writing projects. Teachers have shown me how they take a book such as *Where the Wild Horses Roam* and use it as a springboard for studying geography, math, government, and other subjects. After reading a book such as *Homesteading: Settling America's Heartland,* a student can imagine what it might have been like to be a homesteader, an Indian whose land was being encroached upon, or an animal that had never seen a house before, and write a story incorporating some of the facts in the book. Books such as *Children Save the Rain Forest* can also be the basis for a fund-raising project that empowers children to feel they can do something to help deal with the problems of today.

Selected Titles	
Fire: Friend or Foe	*Biodiversity*
Bold and Bright: Black and White Animals	*Children Save the Rain Forest*
Homesteading: Settling America's Heartland	*Quetzal: Sacred Bird of the Cloud Forest*
In Search of the Maiasaurs	*Prairies*
Mystery of the Lascaux Cave	*West by Covered Wagon*
Secrets of the Ice Man	*Eagles of America*
Wild Turkeys	*Return of the Wolf*
Alex and Friends: Animal Talk, Animal Thinking	*Why Mammals Have Fur*
	Looking at Bears
Apple Trees	*The Vanishing Feast*
Flashy Fantastic Rain Forest Frogs	*Alligators*
Pigeons	*Hugger to the Rescue*
Back to the Wild	

Section I: Learning Experiences and Activities for Utilizing

E-Mail

The role and significance of computers in the classroom is a resource that is just beginning to be tapped. An advantage to planning instruction that utilizes technology is that computers are increasingly available in most schools. Additionally, computers hold tremendous interest for many students. Perhaps the most familiar of the Internet tools is electronic mail, more commonly known as e-mail. E-mail is an increasingly popular method of communication. The availability of e-mail reflects its popularity. Increasingly, school computer labs as well as individual classes are being wired for Internet access. Students may have their own e-mail account at home in addition to opportunities to use e-mail at school. One reality of technology is that in many cases students are both more knowledgeable and more comfortable with it than their teachers and their parents. Teachers should become familiar with the use of e-mail before attempting it with students. Through use, teachers not only will come to see that e-mail can be a useful learning tool, but they will also learn the types of pitfalls that can occur when using this medium. One difficulty with e-mail projects is that teachers and students only have control of the communication that they send out; there are no guarantees that there will be a response. Teachers need to work together if their classes are going to communicate via e-mail to make certain that there is a commitment on both sides.

The immediacy of e-mail is one element that makes it a unique form of communication. Messages can be sent instantaneously to any e-mail address, anywhere in the world. If the recipients are online, they can respond immediately. If not, the mail is then stored in the recipients' accounts by their provider until the recipient retrieves the mail. In the classroom, the main advantage of this immediacy is the ease with which students can share their ideas with other students across the hall, town, the country, or the world. Too many times students view their assignments as meaningless pieces that are written only for the teacher. E-mail creates live, responsive audiences who might respond immediately or within a few hours or a few days.

A second element of e-mail is its format. The address has the appearance of a memorandum:

TO

CC

Subject

While it takes the format of a memo, it is less formal than one. Because it is electronic communication, the communication is quick. Inherent in the informal, conversational nature of e-mail is the danger that the sender may not be communicating effectively. Lack of clarity and an ill-defined context for messages present two of the significant difficulties for e-mail in the classroom.

A third element that makes e-mail unique is the impact that using it has in encouraging many of the most reluctant writers. The reasons for this are complex and varied. The informal nature of the writing has a positive impact on many students. For others the lure is the use of the technology itself. However, it is perhaps the immediate gratification that is possible through instant communication that is most appealing to students.

Students who have difficulty forming their thoughts quickly enough to participate in class discussion can find their voice in the use of e-mail. The anonymity of this tool allows students to express themselves more naturally. Also, students who are constrained by poor handwriting are freed from this limitation when they use a keyboard. With special software adaptations, even physically impaired students are able to communicate effectively through the medium. Moreover, messages do not have to be sent until students are satisfied with them. Students are able to refine and detail their writing. However, they must be assisted in this process or else they may feel the pressure of the immediacy of the medium and rush to complete their thoughts.

Student Reflection and Self-Assessment:

Students can keep an electronic log of their communications. Many e-mail programs automatically save out-going communications. Students can print copies of their messages. Figure 5.1 shows a sample e-mail log.

Examples:

E-mail projects in schools may take many forms. Students in a geography class may communicate with students from Australia, Germany, or any other country that they are studying. A class that is reading the novels of Chris Crutcher might do electronic book reports with classes around the country who have a similar interest. Dialogue journals can be used for discussing science projects with students attending other schools.

In Jake Burdock's class, several of his students found e-mail addresses for their favorite authors on the Internet. They added the authors to their list of e-mail resources.

Sample E-Mail Log

Message	Date Sent	Response Date	Re:
(Person sent to)			

What kinds of information did you contribute to this project?

What kinds of information did you seek?

What kinds of information or assistance did you receive?

How useful was it?

How could you have improved your participation in this project?

What benefits did you gain?

Was this an effective use of your time? Why or Why not.

Figure 5.1

Listservs

A listserv is an electronic discussion group that is organized around a specific common interest of the members. Students participate in a listserv through e-mail, whereby they receive a mass mailing that goes to every member of the listserv. Then they may or may not respond to the list with their own contributions. For example, Book Report is a listserv for students to share their reactions to books that they have read. When a book report is sent out, others who have read the book may choose to respond with other comments or by agreeing with what was sent. Other listservs speak to students' interests in other content areas—for example, math, science, or social studies. A listserv is a place for its members to share information, ask questions, and respond to others. For example, Scholastic Books has a school service on America on Line which covers most content areas. Additionally, they frequently have authors of fiction or nonfiction on-line who respond to student questions. A representative list of listserv addresses can be located in Appendix C.

Guidelines:

- The teacher collects a master list of e-mail addresses for appropriate listservs for the class.
- The teacher demonstrates contacting the listserv.
- The teacher determines the purpose of subscribing to a particular listserv.
- Students are trained to participate on-line.
- The teacher plans specific opportunities for student involvement.

Student Reflection and Self-Assessment:

When students are regularly involved on-line, the teacher should monitor the experience with student checklists or reflections. Another type of necessary assessment is for students to check for the validity of all their findings on the Internet with traditional reference materials.

Example:

Nathan Miller uses several science listservs as an additional source of information for his students. They have become familiar with "checking it on the list." He then has them verify the information they receive in reference books or nonfiction trade books.

CD-ROMs

The level of technological awareness of today's students is often highly sophisticated. Content teachers can augment their classroom resources with content appropriate CD-ROMs. Any CD-ROM contains the equivalent of thousands of pages of documentation. The storage capacity of these disks for the computer replaces whole books. These resources may be encyclopedic in their scope of content or focused on a particular topic, and they may be presented in multimedia fashion.

A CD-ROM has the capacity to include original text that is narrated, still photos, and background or focus music; however, it can also include film clips, audio clips from other sources, graphics, and automated cartoons. The scope of a CD-ROM is limited only by the technology that is available, and that changes constantly.

While the mini-library approach is one function of CD-ROMs, still others are being written to provide audiences with a multimedia approach to a particular topic. These single-subject programs provide the audience with an in-depth examination of the topic. The infusion of film clips, audio, and still pictures creates an immediacy that "hooks" the audience. For a generation of students, many of whom have grown up with computers, this is a logical way to help them to be actively involved in their learning. One of the benefits of an effective CD-ROM is that it provides springboards for students to do further reading about aspects of the topic. Many such programs provide for interactive reading and writing opportunities.

Guidelines:

- The teacher previews all CD-ROMs.
- The teacher sets purposes for using the CD-ROM in the classroom.
- The teacher prepares a user's guide to help students use their time efficiently, e.g., explaining hot words.
- The teacher schedules time for computer use.
- The teacher prepares specific assignments for meaningful interaction with CD-ROMs.

Student Reflection and Self-Assessment:

When using CD-ROMs, students should have opportunities to reflect and assess their value and appropriateness. Figure 5.2 shows a sample instrument.

Self-Assessment

Name _____

Topic of research: _____

Sources used: _____

CD-ROMs: _____   Books: _____

What were the major concepts you learned from the CD-ROMs?

Which concepts were confirmed by information in books or other print materials you've read?

Were there any major discrepancies between the CD-ROMs and print materials? If so, what were they? How did you reconcile the differences?

What were the advantages to using CD-ROMs? What were the disadvantages?

Figure 5.2

Example:

An excellent example of a focused CD-ROM is *Images from the Holocaust* (1996) by A. Nadine Burke. In this multimedia presentation, Burke presents a background of the times; identifies major figures, Nazis, rescuers, and survivors; explores the issues of the times; and shows the major events. It is a powerful, yet enlightening introduction to the period. The CD-ROM also examines the varied experiences that Holocaust victims and survivors endured (hiding, fleeing, living in concentration camps, among other type of experiences). These images of survival or death parallel sections of the literature anthology by the same name that the CD-ROM was designed to accompany, *Images from the Holocaust* by Brown, Stephens, and Rubin, 1996.

Class Web Pages

One of the most rapidly growing sources of information dissemination is the Internet. "Surfing the web" has become a daily experience for millions of Americans. A web page may be seen as a combination of information with built-in indices included. One typical type of web page provides its reader with several brief paragraphs of information. Within the paragraphs are "hot words," usually in bright blue. The reader clicks on these words to go to another page where there will be more in-depth information. Another approach is for the first page to be a catalogue of what will follow, again with hot words. Depending on the software used to create a web paper, the graphics and page design may be quite sophisticated.

Web page design is one way of capitalizing on students' interest and knowledge of technology that has numerous benefits. This type of activity allows those students who have the technological skills to assist the teacher and the other class members as "technology consultants." In doing a class web page, teachers can involve students for whom the traditional learning format seems boring or irrelevant.

The teacher begins the process by setting purposes for the web page. It needs to be a true merger between content, student-learning-through-doing, and technology. All of these components contribute to the overall meaning and value of this experience. This experience can be an excellent learning experience when carefully conceptualized and systematically planned.

Guidelines:

- The teacher models a web page that reflects course concepts.
- At the conclusion of a class unit, the students brainstorm what to include on the unit web page.
- All students are expected to participate in two groups, the first concerned with content and the second concerned with web page production.
- Student groups are established to work on the content.
- Each group determines the format of their content.
- Class member select one of the following production teams to work on: technology consultants, editorial board, keyboarding experts, graphic designers.
- The whole class meets for consensus-building to determine a common format.
- Content groups make decisions about the subject matter of their section and meet with the technology and design groups to determine how to go from conceptualization to finished product.
- Content groups turn work over to the editorial board.
- The editorial board makes appropriate revisions and then gives the work to the keyboarding group.
- The technology consultants and graphic designers work with the keyboarding experts to prepare the project.

- The teacher and class members review the final draft, checking for accuracy, clarity, and overall effectiveness.
- Final editing and revisions are made.
- Class page is submitted to the server as a web page.

Student Reflection and Self-Assessment:

Students write a reflective paper about their involvement. They talk about their participation in both the content group and the production group. They do a self-evaluation and support their responses.

Example:

After reading *Dogsong* (1985) by Gary Paulsen, a seventh grade English class decided that they wanted to know more about dogsled racing. Individual class members read several other books on the topic and became even more interested in the Iditarod. They then looked for information on the Internet where they found a number of web sites. The students decided that they had lots of good information about books on the subject and they wanted to put up a web page to reflect the work they had been doing. They used hot words to direct their readers to the other sites on the topic.

Simulations

A simulation is a classroom representation of an issue, situation, or problem presented to students for their analysis and response. A simulation, usually presented in the form of a scenario, provides opportunities for students to make real-life connections and utilize their learning to address the conditions and issues presented in it. Simulations are interactive instructional experiences that help students become involved in utilizing their content learning. A simulation can reduce complex problems or situations to manageable elements, as well as increase the student's ability to apply principles. In doing a simulation, students assume roles that may help to sensitize them to another person's role in life. Assuming a role may also facilitate student understanding of their current roles or help them to understand roles that may affect their life but that they may never assume. Moreover, in doing a simulation, students have the opportunity to assume new roles that may help prepare them for the future.

Guidelines:

- Determine the desired purposes and outcomes of the simulation.
- Develop a scenario for the simulation that includes all pertinent information such as conditions, time period, and geographical location.
- Identify key roles for student participants, whether as individuals, groups, organizations, or institutions.
- Develop role cards with descriptions including all relevant information about each of the roles. These may be kept on index cards or in computer-generated data bases.
- Determine and allocate appropriate class time for responding to the scenario.
- Present the scenario to the class.
- Introduce the roles.
- Either assign or allow students to select roles.
- Provide organizational time as part of doing the simulation.
- Debrief—whole class and individual (see Figure 5.3 for a sample debriefing form).

Students Reflection and Self-Assessment:

Sample Simulation Debriefing Form

What did you learn from the experience?

How did it have an impact on your thinking about [specify the particular issue, situation, or problem]?

What was effective about the experience?

What would you change about the experience?

In what other ways might you learn more about [specify the particular issue, situation, or problem]?

Figure 5.3

Examples:

Simulations have wide application in all content area classrooms. They can help students to discover concepts, ideas, and principles. For example, an effective math simulation is "A Day Without Numbers." In science, students plan strategies to protect the wildlife after an oil spill. In history, the class could simulate the siege of Vicksburg. In economics, they might simulate the mediation of a world-wide oil crisis. English students might simulate an advertising campaign covering Internet, radio, television, and print media. In a sociology class, students can hold a mock court trial for cases of welfare abuse. Simulations are adaptable in every content area and create opportunities for real student involvement.

Published simulations are a valuable resource for teachers. INTERACT has simulations in a wide variety of subject areas and grade levels. Catalogs of this material are available at the following address:

INTERACT
1825 Gillespie Way #101
El Cajon, California 92020-1095
(616) 448-1474 or (800) 359-0961   e-mail: teachers@interact-simulations.com

Another publisher of simulations is Teacher Created Materials, whose address is:
Teacher Created Materials
6421 Industry Way
Westminster, CA 92683
(800) 662-4321   www.teachercreated.com

Projects

A wide range of activities often falls under the general heading of "projects." The major purpose of all projects, however, is usually similar. That is, a project should provide students with opportunities to utilize their knowledge and skills with as much independence as possible and to investigate and problem-solve in as lifelike a situation as possible, resulting in an end product. While most projects result in a tangible product, other projects may result in a performance or a report describing action that was taken to solve a problem. Projects may be conducted individually, in pairs, or small groups, but occasionally they involve a whole class. Projects can be valuable learning experiences, but the element of choice is crucial to the success of any project. While the teacher decides the parameters, students must have both the freedom and responsibility to make a number of important decisions and choices.

Guidelines:

- The teacher establishes purposes, time frames, standards for evaluation, and other parameters, including whether students will work individually, in pairs, or in small groups and what process, abilities, and skills must be demonstrated during the project.
- Students select projects with teacher guidance and approval.
- Students plan their projects, including a timeline for completion with checkpoints along the way. The projects should be reasonable in terms of the amount of time they will take to complete and the cost of supplies, if any.
- The teacher schedules regular checkpoint times for students to reflect upon their progress and to seek feedback and assistance from their peers. The projects should involve real learning experiences, including decision-making and problem-solving, not busy work.
- Students organize, develop, and complete their projects. Projects are presented for the whole class.
- Students conclude their projects with a final self-assessment.

Student Reflections and Self-Assessment:

Sample reflection form to use during project checkpoints

1. What have I accomplished on the project during (specify a time period)?
2. What problems am I having with my project?
3. What should I do to try to solve those problems?
4. What am I planning to do next on the project?

Sample self-assessment form to use upon completion of the project

1. What did I learn about (specify topic or content) from doing this project?
2. What did I learn about myself and the way I work from doing this project?
3. What are the strong points and weak points of my final product?
4. What advice would I give to someone else before they do a project?

Example:

After reading *Follow the Sun* by Paul Pitts, Gary Hobert had his social studies class research and collect pictures and information about Navaho culture, including rituals, reservation life, arts and crafts, and beliefs. As the students collected information and worked on their group projects, the whole class researched and built a life-size hogan in the classroom. The final group projects were displayed around the hogan.

Problem-Solving

Teaching students to use problem-solving approaches is an important process in helping them become independent, lifelong learners in all content areas. While some teachers may initially teach problem-solving with contrived problems, the goal is for students to use problem-solving approaches with the real problems they face in their lives. Although contrived problems may help students begin to understand the complex thinking processes in problem-solving, there is the real danger that students will come away from such activities believing that problems can be solved by following a step-by-step recipe, rather than understanding the cyclical nature of problem-solving.

Guidelines:

We include three approaches to problem-solving. The first approach, by Clark and Starr (1996, pp. 241–242), is based on the work of John Dewey.

1. The learner becomes aware of the problem.
2. The learner defines and delimits the problem.
3. The learner gathers evidence that may help solve the problem.
4. The learner forms a hypothesis of what the solution to the problem is.
5. The learner tests the hypothesis.
6. The learner successfully solves the problem, or repeats steps 3, 4, and 5, or 4 and 5, until the problem is solved, or gives up.

Joan Countryman (1992, p. 59) describes a second approach to problem-solving in her book, *Writing to Learn Mathematics: Strategies That Work, K-12.*

1. Experiencing the phenomenon.
2. Stating the problem.
3. Constructing a mathematical model.
4. Manipulating algebraic statements.
5. Stating a solution.
6. Interpreting the solution in a mathematical context.
7. Interpreting the solution in the real world.

The third approach is described by Cangelosi (1992, pp. 75–76) in his book on teaching mathematics, but is not limited to solving mathematical problems.

1. The person is confronted with a puzzling question or questions (e.g., regarding how to do something or explain a phenomenon) that he or she wants to answer.
2. The person clarifies the question or questions posed by the problem, often in terms of more specific questions about quantities.

3. The principal variable or variables to be solved are identified.

4. The situation is visualized so that relevant relations involving the principal variable or variables are identified and possible solution designs are considered.

5. The solution plan is finalized, including (a) selection of measurements (i.e. how data are to be collected), (b) identification of relations to establish, and (c) selection of algorithms to execute.

6. Data are gathered (i.e., measurements taken).

7. The processes, formulas, or algorithms are executed with the data.

8. Results of the executions of processes, formulas, or algorithms are interpreted to shed light on the original question or questions.

9. The person makes a value judgment regarding the original question or questions.

All problem-solving approaches have many elements in common. Our recommendation is that teachers find a problem-solving approach and adapt it to fit their content area and the level and needs of their students. What is most important is that students are taught an approach and then given ample opportunities to use it

Student Reflections and Self-Assessment:

Students benefit from having opportunities to reflect upon their use of problem-solving approaches. Figure 5.4 provides a sample student reflection and self-assessment form.

Problem-Solving Reflection

(1)   What is the easiest part of the problem-solving approach for me? the most difficult?

(2)   What do I need to work on to improve my ability to problem-solve?

(3)   How can I use the problem-solving approach in other situations outside of this class?

Figure 5.4

Example:

In her unit on ecology, Opal Walker uses newspaper clippings of environmental problems as the basis for having her students seek solutions. She has developed a modified problem-solving approach that helps her students generate possible answers for environmental issues they're studying.

Writing for Publication

Writing for Publication is a powerful way for students to utilize their learning in every content area. Noden and Vacca state that: "Publishing reaffirms. It communicates that writing is important, meaningful, and valuable. It allows students to feel the excitement of seeing an audience respond to their written words, and enables them to travel into the minds of other students, exploring the common bond of human communication that lies at the core of all writing" (1994, p. 160). In too many situations, however, students engage *only* in functional writing, that is, writing without composing, such as notetaking and some of the strategies we have described in Chapters 3 and 4. While functional writing is an important tool for learning, students also need opportunities to engage in meaningful, extended writing in which they communicate with others their ideas and insights; the knowledge they've developed and the connections they've made; and their interest and excitement about things of importance to them. But, as Strickland and Stickland state, "In order for any type of writing to be a tool to facilitate learning, however, the learner must view the writing as purposeful. Regurgitation of what the teacher or the textbook says is not using writing as a means of thinking and learning" (1993, p. 107). Writing for Publication—that is, writing something for someone else to read—is purposeful and meaningful writing involving a high degree of thinking and learning.

Why write? Lucy Calkins offers the following answer:

> We'll read and write to understand, to probe a subject, to pursue our questions, to figure out what we know, to organize our learning, to solicit new knowledge, to clarify our ideas, to feel, to remember, to plan . . . We will also, at some point, begin to read and write as experts on a subject. Our investigations will continue, but we'll also become teachers of a subject. We'll write letters to members of Congress and journalists and people who need to know about the subject. We'll sketch out plans for speeches and workshops. We'll write brochures, manuals, editorials, personal essays, articles, historical fiction, poems, announcements. (1994, p. 478)

For writers there is a need that can only be met through writing, but for many others, it is a laborious and even painful process. Frequently, we compound the problem in schools by using writing as an academic exercise that has little connection to students, their lives, and their interests. We are using the term Writing for Publication to indicate the need to provide students with opportunities to do committed writing, writing that they have an interest in and writing that will be read by a variety of audiences. Meaningful writing provides students with opportunities to apply the meanings that they have constructed. Writing is an appropriate vehicle for helping students utilize what they have learned to solve problems and understand the meaning of their learning in contexts beyond the classroom.

Teachers sometimes shy away from Writing for Publication because they think it involves lengthy, complex, and costly procedures. In reality, Writing for Publication is more a philosophy than a set of procedures and it encompasses a wide range of types of publishing. These vary from something as simple as a students posting their work on a bulletin board for others to read to something as complicated as students producing a school newspaper or magazine. The significant component in all Writing for Publication activities is *audience*: that is, students write for an audience beyond the teacher or themselves.

Examples:

The following list provides a starting point for ideas for Writing for Publication:

Writing on Display: Writing displayed on bulletin boards, in show cases, in waiting rooms, or accompanying projects, experiments, and displays

"Coffee House" Writing: Work that is intended to be read aloud in an informal setting

Public Letters: Letters to the editor, public officials, businesses, organizations, and community publications

Writing Contests: Writing submitted to local, regional, state, and national competitions

Publications: Writing and producing newspapers, magazines, anthologies, class books, pamphlets, brochures, flyers, newsletters, manuals, technical reports, case studies, fiction, short stories, poetry, informational books, and picture books

Writing for Performance: Plays, songs, skits, television programs, documentaries, films

Electronic Writing: E-mail writing partners, web pages, CD-ROMs, HyperStudio

Among the modes of writing that we encourage students to use are *informative*, *expressive*, *persuasive*, and *imaginative*. These modes provide a broadly based foundation for students to do a variety of types of writing for a range of audiences, and even more importantly, give them the opportunity to write for a number of purposes.

Informative writing, also called expository writing, has a fundamental content focus and is used by students when they write to inform or share with others knowledge, information, and ideas. Examples of informative writing include reports, news stories, technical reports, lab reports, case studies, comparison/contrast papers, historical/biographical sketches, among other types of content-centered explorations. Informative writing should provide students with a range of opportunities to synthesize and apply the meanings they have constructed.

Expressive writing (or personal narratives) reflects the personal experiences, feelings, and thoughts of the writer. Students express their views and reactions through letters, personal observations, diaries, journals, and position papers, among other types of expressive writing. In expressive writing, students have the opportunity to tell their own stories.

Persuasive writing makes a case. It uses a line of reasoning to persuade the reader of the writer's point of view. When writing persuasively, students logically develop a position to influence the reader. The forms for this type of writing include reviews of books, films, software, television, and plays; editorials; point/counterpoint; letters to the editor; and position papers; among others.

Imaginative writing encompasses the range of creative writing. Among the creative experiences with writing are the following: short stories, poems, play scenes, science fiction, fantasies, cartoons, historical recreations, and dialogues, among others.

In the following Author Perspective, we hear from Janet Bode, an award-winning author who has given voice to many young people in her nonfiction. She explores major issues that have an impact on today's youth by interviewing them as well as experts in the field.

An Author's Perspective
JANET BODE

Janet Bode lives in New York City and travels exten-
sively. She is an in-the-trenches researcher, chroni-
cling the lives of kids around the country. "What's
working for you and what isn't?" she asks them.
"What have you learned that you can pass on to oth-
ers?" Ultimately her books are collections of their sto-
ries. In their own words, in their own way, today's
adolescents speak frankly to her about the reality of
being caught in the cross-hairs of social change and
their strategies for succeeding.

Janet Bode's books have received numerous
awards from such organizations as the American Library Association, the National Council
for the Social Studies, and the International Reading Association; and her book Different
Worlds: Interracial and Cross-Cultural Dating *inspired a CBS-TV Schoolbreak Special. She*
has also written two adult trade nonfiction books, as well as articles for various periodicals,
including The New York Times, Village Voice, Glamour, *and* Cosmopolitan.

When I was thirteen, someone gave me a diary for Christmas. Although clothes were more what I wanted, I decided to start keeping a daily journal anyway. By the time I put down my pen, I had chronicled my life to its nineteenth year.

Today I appreciate that I began to record teenagers' stories with my own. In the dozen plus books I've created, I'm now the quiet presence. Their collected voices are the strength, as they discuss how their lives intersect with a particular issue—from eating disorders in *Food Fight* to warring siblings in *Truce*. The American Library Association, the International Reading Association and the National Council for Social Studies, among others, consistently select my titles for awards. Better yet, the books generate mail from readers across the country. The stories, they tell me, resonate with the reality they know.

For me, having books published has a similar feel to growing up in a large family. While each one is a part of the whole, each also has a life of its own. *Dif-*ferent Worlds: Interracial and Cross-Cultural Dating *inspired a CBS-TV Schoolbreak Special that became a finalist for the NAACP Humanitas Award and a nominee for four daytime Emmys. *Heartbreak and Roses: Real Life Stories of Troubled Love* gave me the chance to go on "Oprah" to talk about teen dating violence. And *Trust and Betrayal: Real Life Stories of Friends and Enemies* meant I could widen the debate on peer pressure to include the often ignored point, how exactly do you build solid friendships in the first place?

I think of myself as an advocate for teenagers—the books, my contribution to helping adolescents make choices and, in the process, open doors into the world beyond them.

I want to connect with readers, erode the widely-held misconception that nonfiction is by definition boring. Instead, these books both speak their language and carry them along with the same intensity as good fiction. They see, too, the flexibility of my format. They can start reading on page one and go through the chapters in sequence. Or they can pick and choose what they especially want to read and in what order, as in a periodical.

I hope they also discover that information can be conveyed in a range of ways—as poetry, essays, original surveys, quotations from secondary sources, first-person stories told in words alone or with words and pictures (often created by my partner, reporter/cartoonist, Stan Mack).

Beyond that I want to provoke readers, challenge them to think about themselves, how they conduct their lives and how they measure up to their peers nationwide. And finally, for those who feel most isolated, I want them to come away with a sense of hope, knowing that they are *not* alone, but also that others have found solutions to the same life problems.

Selected Titles

Beating the Odds: Stories of Unexpected Achievers (illustrated by Stan Mack)
The Colors of Freedom: Immigrant Stories
Death Is Hard To Live With: Teenagers Talk About How They Cope With Loss, (illustrated by Stan Mack)
Food Fight: A Guide to Eating Disorders for Preteens and Their Parents
Hard Time: A Real Life Look at Juvenile Crime and Violence (co-author, Stan Mack)

Heartbreak and Roses: Real Life Stories of Troubled Love (co-author, Stan Mack)
Kids Still Have Kids: Talking About Teen Pregnancy (illustrated by Stan Mack and Ida Marx Blue Spruce)
Truce: Ending the Sibling War
Voices of Rape (illustrated by Ida Marx Blue Spruce)

Section II: Content Literacy Strategies for Utilizing

STRATEGY: ACTION with FACTS: A Planning Guide

Component:	Content Literacy Process:	Organizing for Instruction:
Initiating Constructing Utilizing	Reading Writing Speaking Listening Viewing	Individual Pairs Small Group Whole Class

Description:

ACTION with FACTS: A Planning Guide (see Figure 5.5) provides students with a strategy for planning, organizing, and completing projects and other long-term class assignments. An important aspect of utilizing is providing students with opportunities to develop independence in their learning. Students need assistance in developing the skills of independent work, but without a rigid prescription that doesn't allow them to make meaningful decisions. ACTION with FACTS: A Planning Guide provides structure with a flexible format that encourages student creativity, responsibility, and accountability.

Procedures:

- The teacher presents the project or other long-term assignment to the class.
- Students are encouraged to ask questions about it.
- Then the teacher writes on the board: ACTION with FACTS, and distributes the planning guide.
- The teacher explains and models the ACTION portion of the guide.
- Students are given assistance to use the planning guide individually, in pairs, or in small groups.
- After the students have been working on their projects or other long-term assignments for a few days, the teacher introduces the FACTS portion of the guide and explains and models how to use it.
- Near the due date for the completed project or long-term assignment, the teacher refers the students again to the FACTS portion of the guide.

Variations:

- Many teachers find that students have the most difficulty establishing timelines and breaking the work down into smaller tasks. Some teachers facilitate this by establishing "Checkpoint Dates." Students must demonstrate that they have accomplished certain things by these dates.

- Several of the strategies described in chapter 4 such as note taking, data charts, and other graphic organizers are valuable tools for students when working on projects or other long-term assignments.

Example:

ACTION with FACTS

ACTION = Use this part of the guide to help you plan and begin the assignment or project.

A = Assignment.   Carefully read and think about the assignment (or project). Ask questions about it.

C = Create.   Create a positive mental image of you working on and completing the assignment.

T = Timeline.   Establish a timeline for completing the assignment. Start with the due date and work backwards.

I = Ideas.   Brainstorm ideas. Record and think about them. Decide which ones to use.

O = Organize.   Organize the work to be done. Break it up into smaller tasks.

N = Notes.   Write notes to yourself with what you need to do next.

FACTS = Use this part of the guide at specific checkpoints while you work on the assignment and at the completion of the assignment.

F = Feedback.   Have you asked others for feedback on the work you've done so far?

A = Adjust.   Have you adjusted your tasks and timeline as needed?

C = Contribute.   How does your work contribute to your knowledge and understanding of the topic? What can it contribute to others?

T = Think.   Think about your completed assignment or finished project. What are its strengths and weaknesses?

S = Self-assessment.   What have you learned from this entire experience? What are you most proud of? What would you do differently another time?

Figure 5.5

STRATEGY: RAFT

Component:	Content Literacy Process:	Organizing for Instruction:
Initiating Constructing Utilizing	Reading Writing Speaking Listening Viewing	Individual Pairs Small Group Whole Class

Description:

RAFT (Vanderventer, 1979) is a 4-step process to help students make decisions about their writing. Writing for publication is a powerful learning experience highly recommended for the utilizing phase of the instructional framework because it gives students an opportunity to demonstrate their understanding of content material with a polished product for a real audience. Students who have been writing primarily for themselves, using such devices as journals, logs, and notetaking, need help to plan for writing for an audience. RAFT guides students in considering questions about the author's role or voice, audience, format, and topic.

R = Role of the writer.
   What is my role as the writer? (e.g., a student, an expert, a reporter, a first person observer of history)
A = Audience to whom the writing is directed.
   For whom am I writing? (e.g., peers, teacher, administration, public, legislators)
F = Format in which the writing will be done.
   What form should I use for this writing? (e.g., journal, letter, essay, dialogue, poem, laboratory report)
T = Topic about which the writing will be done.
   What topic will I write about?

Procedures:

- The teacher presents RAFT and appropriate examples for the content area.
- Using brainstorming, the class practices generating and discussing responses to the four questions until everyone understands what must be taken into consideration with each one.
- Then students, individually, in pairs, or in small groups use RAFT as they plan their writing for publication.

Variations:

- Because the topic is so important and generally influences all the other decisions, teachers frequently recommend that, when students use RAFT, they do a quick overview of the four questions and then consider the T (topic) first.
- Once students are comfortable with RAFT, they can exercise a high degree of independence in its use.

Example:

In her social studies class, Mary Lou Storey had her students do a RAFTing experience during their unit on Colonial America. She created the chart shown in Figure 5.6 for her students. They were to select one item from each of the first three columns, but then create their own topic for the writing.

Role	Audience	Format	Topic
sailor	home	editorial	student choice
pilgrim	community	letter	
Gov. Bradford	shipping company	diary	
young child	minister	news article	
female Pilgrim	self	narrative of the trip	

Figure 5.6

STRATEGY: Discussion Continuum

Component:	Content Literacy Process:	Organizing for Instruction:
Initiating	Reading	Individual
Constructing	Writing	Pairs
Utilizing	Speaking	Small Group
	Listening	Whole Class
	Viewing	

Description:

The discussion continuum (Stephens & Brown, 1994) provides a structured format for whole class discussion of a topic. It is particularly useful during the utilizing component of the instructional framework, when the teacher is attempting to have students apply their knowledge to a particular situation.

> The discussion continuum is a strategy for involving **all** students in a lively discussion. The teacher draws a continuum on the board with opposing statements at either end point. As the students enter the classroom, they write their initials somewhere along the continuum on the spot which best specifies their own position on the issue. During the discussion, the students explain their positions, often using references from their reading to back up their points. The only rules are that everyone must have a chance to speak before anyone can speak for a second time and that all positions must be listened to respectfully. (p. 681)

Procedures:

- The most efficient way to teach the discussion continuum is to use it with the whole class, with a high-interest topic for which students hold a wide range of positions. The teacher should emphasize that everyone must respond at least once, that all positions will be listened to respectfully, and that after everyone has spoken, students may change their positions on the continuum and then speak again.

- Initially, the teacher may want to structure the discussion so that students representing views at opposite ends of the continuum alternate speaking. Generally, once students get involved, they take over the discussion themselves and soon are responding to each other rather than using the teacher as the person who must keep the discussion going.

- To ensure that students apply the knowledge they have been learning to the issue on the discussion continuum, provide the students with the issue several days in advance of the class discussion. Have them prepare support for their position from sources they've been studying, using note cards or data charts (see Chapter 4 for a description).

Variations:

- The discussion continuum can serve as an effective springboard for writing where students explain several different positions on an issue or try to persuade readers to take a certain position.

- Once students understand how to use the discussion continuum, they can develop their own issues in small groups.

- Some teachers use the discussion continuum first as an initiating strategy before the students have studied a particular topic, and then again, afterwards, to help them see how information can help us to make more informed decisions.

Example:

Ervin Woodbury used the discussion continuum shown in Figure 5.7 in his American Government class.

The government should
regulate the Internet for
content.

The government
should not regulate the
Internet for content.

Figure. 5.7

STRATEGY: Ask the Expert

Component:	Content Literacy Process:	Organizing for Instruction:
Initiating	Reading	Individual
Constructing	Writing	Pairs
Utilizing	Speaking	Small Group
	Listening	Whole Class
	Viewing	

Description:

An important aspect of utilizing is providing students with opportunities to be independent learners. This strategy, Ask the Expert, encourages students to become the class authority on a particular topic.

Procedures:

- The teacher models researching specific topics for in-depth information using a wide range of resource materials.
- The class members brainstorm a list of topics related to a particular theme or area currently being studied.
- Each student selects a topic or offers an alternate topic to research in order to become the expert.
- The teacher helps direct the research by providing materials.
- The students research the topics and prepare to share the findings with the class.
- In the classroom, the teacher has a display, entitled Ask the Expert, where the students are recognized along with the topic they have explored.

Variation:

- Some teachers have files of the reports that students have done in loose leaf notebooks as a resource for other students.

Examples:

Charlene Williams used this strategy in her American history class to help students gain a sense of the human side of history. For example, her students have become experts on the statistics and types of diseases during the Civil War; life in the Plymouth Colony; comparisons of major stock market declines; the role of young people in the Civil Rights Movement; as well as other topics.

Judson Mathews uses this strategy to have interested students do author studies for his English class. The author profiles are kept in a notebook where students can read them or even add new information that they have discovered.

Strategy: I-Search Paper

Component:	Content Literacy Process:	Organizing for Instruction:
Initiating	Reading	Individual
Constructing	Writing	Pairs
Utilizing	Speaking	Small Group
	Listening	Whole Class
	Viewing	

Description:

The I-Search Paper (Macrorie, 1988) is a more personalized form of research than the typical research paper. It allows students to become personally involved with their topic through a customized search for information that goes beyond the typical read-and-regurgitate format to include interviews and other sources, to use first-person in their writing, and to describe their search as a significant part of the final paper. As a utilizing experience, the I-Search Paper (see Figure 5.8) enables students to apply content knowledge they have already developed and to use problem-solving as they search for new sources of information.

Procedures:

- The students, individually, in pairs, or in small groups, choose a topic. The topic should have personal interest and appeal and be something that students genuinely want to know more about.
- The students decide where to search for more information, particularly focusing on experts or knowledgeable people that they might interview. They design interview questions based on what they are interested in learning more about or questions they have on the topic.
- The students conduct the interviews and seek other sources of information.
- The students write their papers as a narrative of their search for more information and answers to questions they had on a topic with high personal interest.

Variations:

- Frequently teachers need to show students how to develop appropriate interview questions and techniques.
- Teachers have found that several of the strategies described in Chapter 4, such as note taking, data charts, and other graphic organizers, are valuable tools for students working with the I-Search format.
- The Taking ACTION with FACTS: A Planning Guide strategy described in this chapter on page 144 works well with students who need more help in structuring and organizing themselves to do I-Search Papers.

Example:

The I-Search Paper (Macrorie, 1988)

Step 1: Choose a topic.

Step 2: Carry-out the search.

Step 3: Conduct the interview(s).

Step 4: Write the paper, including these four categories of information:
    a. What you did and did not know about the topic prior to conducting the search for information.

    b. Why you decided to research this particular topic.

    c. A description of your search.

    d. Describe and discuss what you learned.

Step 5: Provide a list of all sources.

Figure 5.8

STRATEGY: Ethical Choices

Component:	Content Literacy Process:	Organizing for Instruction:
Initiating Constructing Utilizing	Reading Writing Speaking Listening Viewing	Individual Pairs Small Group Whole Class

Description:

 Most content areas have controversial issues in their curriculum. This strategy, Ethical Choices, is designed to provide students with opportunities to address difficult topics and take a position. Providing students with opportunities to search for answers helps them to utilize the meanings that they have constructed.

Procedures:

- The teacher begins by introducing an issue that has a number of opposing positions.
- Students write a brief position paper based on their current and prior knowledge of the issue.
- The teacher presents an overview of the major positions in an unbiased, factual way.
- The teacher presents either a packet of reading material on the subject or an annotated list, with information to help students read balanced accounts.
- Students are to read a minimum of two selections from the packet or list representing at least two different perspectives.
- Students then complete the issues map (see Figure 5.9), listing arguments pro and con.
- Students weigh the arguments and then take an informed stand (the resolution), supported by documentation.
- Students compare their original stand with the new one, explaining why it did or why it did not change.

Variation:

- Some teachers use this strategy as a whole class activity with the students writing their initial reaction and then the teacher presenting the opposing perspectives for class discussion. The final stage is for students to weigh the evidence and then vote for the position that they find most appropriate.

Examples:

In his health class, Ned Fisher has his students research the ethical positions and choices in the physician-assisted suicide issue. They use an issue map to help them organize their information (see Figure 5.9).

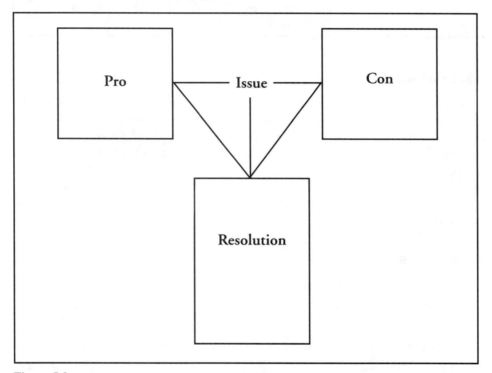

Figure 5.9

In Erin O'Reilly's English class, students read Caroline Cooney's *Driver's Ed* (1994)and Todd Strasser's *The Accident* (1998). The student-directed discussion focused on some of the ethical concerns that these books raise, i.e., drinking and driving, thoughtless pranks with serious consequences, blame and responsibility, among others. She used issue mapping to help her students discuss ethical choices.

STRATEGY: Project Journal

Component:	Content Literacy Process:	Organizing for Instruction:
Initiating Constructing Utilizing	Reading Writing Speaking Listening Viewing	Individual Pairs Small Group Whole Class

Description:

A project journal is a device used by students to plan, organize, develop, and implement their ideas for group work. It is the place where they can keep a record of their on-going work on a project. For pairs and small groups, it also provides a check for completing assignments. "Students have a written account that they can reflect on and use to make judgments and evaluations. The project journal is, therefore, useful in providing a structure in which students may work. It also facilitates an understanding of the mutuality of responsibility for group projects" (Brown, Phillips, and Stephens, 1993, p. 70).

Procedures:

- The teacher and students generate a format for the journal (see Figure 5.10).
- In small groups or pairs, roles and responsibilities are identified and
- selected.
- Roles are randomly assigned initially and subsequently alternated.
- One group member (or all members on a rotating basis) serves as the group scribe to record progress and participation, raise questions, and plan future directions.
- All group members do a reflection entry at the end of the project, including assessment sheets on the contributions.

Variation:

- The primary variation for the project journal is when students are working independently. In this case, students record their own actions and progress.

Examples:

Sample Project Journal Page

Date: _____   Class Period: _____

Team Roles/Student Names _____

Group leader _____

Recorder/ Scribe _____

Researcher _____

Assistant _____

   Tasks to accomplish   Accomplished

1.

2.

3.

Reflecting and assessing:

Today we were successful at:

Next we need to:

Figure 5.10

Students in Mary Davis' seventh grade English class selected one of seven novels to read. The students grouped themselves according to the book they selected. In these groups, they created an ad campaign "to sell" their book to the other members of the class. In their project journals they recorded their ideas for the campaign and the roles each member played.

STRATEGY: Observational Notebook

Component:	Content Literacy Process:	Organizing for Instruction:
Initiating	Reading	Individual
Constructing	Writing	Pairs
Utilizing	Speaking	Small Group
	Listening	Whole Class
	Viewing	

Description:

- An observational notebook is a place where students record what they see or hear. This strategy is designed for broad observational recordings as a means of stimulating student curiosity. The observational notebook can be adapted for use in any discipline where students are expected to do observations.

- Using an observational notebook encourages students to use writing for themselves and to establish the habit of writing in their notebooks.

- The notebook can be loosely or more tightly structured. For example, a teacher might assign her students to observe and make comments about cloud formations for several days. Another teacher might have students use their notebooks for collecting pieces of dialogue that they can use in stories that they will be writing.

Procedures:

- The teacher provides an observational experience for students and models how to write observations.

- Students then record their own observations of another brief experience.

- As a class, they share and compare their observations, looking for commonalties and differences.

Variation:

- Some teachers have students use their observational notebooks for classroom observations such as demonstrations, group presentations, or oral reports.

Examples:

Mitchell Thomas, an 8th grade science teacher, began his unit on the environment by assigning each class member the task of jotting down any observations they had over a weekend about how the local environment was being used, abused, or helped in their community. All class members recorded their observations in a notebook. Students shared their observations, but initially they recognized only the obvious (such as a leak from the local chemical company or the efforts of local groups to reinforce the banks of the rivers in the area to minimize erosion from storms and from recreational boating). As the class studied types of pollution, sources of environmental hazards, and ecological renewal efforts, their observations were more informed and their comments in their notebooks were more detailed.

David Keith assigned his geometry students to teams whose purpose was to explore geometry shapes. The groups designated a leader, who then drew the name of a shape from a jar. The assignment was for each group member to look for their shape in everyday objects for the next three days. The students recorded their findings in their observational notebooks using a format specified by the teacher (see Figure 5.11). Later the class discussed their observations.

Observations

Student_____   Shape _____

Date _____   Location _____

Size _____

Functional? How? _____

Ornamental? How? _____

Date _____   Location _____

Size _____

Functional? How? _____

Ornamental? How? _____

Date _____   Location _____

Size _____

Functional? How? _____

Ornamental? How? _____

General Observations:

Figure 5.11

References

Brown, J., Phillips, L., & Stephens, E. (1993). *Toward literacy: Theory and applications for teaching writing in the content areas.* Belmont, CA: Wadsworth Publishers, ITP.

Brown, J. E., Stephens, E. C., & Rubin, J. E. (1996). *Images from the Holocaust: A literature anthology.* Lincolnwood, IL: NTC Publishing Group.

Burke, A. N. (1996). *Images from the Holocaust: CD-ROM for Windows.* Lincolnwood, IL: NTC Publishing Group.

Calkins, L. (1986, 1994). *The art of teaching writing,* (new edition). Portsmouth, NH: Heinemann.

Cangelosi, J. S. (1992). *Teaching mathematics in secondary and middle school: Research-based approaches.* New York: Macmillan.

Clark, L. H. and Starr, I. S. (1996). *Secondary and middle school teaching methods,* (7th edition). Englewood Cliffs, NJ: Prentice-Hall.

Cooney, C. (1994). *Driver's ed.* New York: Delacorte Press.

Countryman, J. (1992). *Writing to learn mathematics: Strategies that work, K-12.* Portsmouth, NH: Heinemann.

Macrorie, K. (1988). *The I-search paper.* Portsmouth, NH: Heinemann.

Noden, H. R., & Vacca, R. T. (1994). *Whole language in middle and secondary classrooms.* New York: HarperCollins.

Paulsen, G. (1985). *Dogsong.* New York: Scholastic.

Stephens, E. C., & Brown, J. E. (May 1994). The discussion continuum. *The Journal of Reading, 37* (6), 680–681.

Strasser, T. (1988). *The accident.* New York: Dell.

Strickland, K., & Strickland, J. (1993). *Uncovering the curriculum: Whole language in secondary and postsecondary classrooms.* Portsmouth, NH: Boynton/Cook.

Vanderventer, N. (Winter 1979). RAFT: A process to structure prewriting. *Highway One: A Canadian Journal of Language Experience, 26.*

CHAPTER 6

Literature in All Classrooms

Today's students can be a difficult audience; they are used to flipping a switch and having a world of entertainment at their command, whether from television, video games, or the Internet. But then they enter our classrooms and we expect that they will be engaged in our subject matter by reading a large, heavy textbook. "The idea of an isolated text no longer makes sense as children today are exposed to more fluid forms of information transfer" (El-Hindi, 1998, p. 694). Students need a visually exciting and intellectually rich environment to capture their attention and involve them in active and meaningful learning. We believe that one of the most effective ways to accomplish this is by using literature, including trade books (fiction and nonfiction published for a mass audience) and a wide-range of other print sources from newspapers to magazines to cyber texts. In this chapter, we address the following questions that teachers have as they seek to use literature in all classrooms:

Why should I use literature and other print materials in my content classes?

How do I establish appropriate purposes for using literature and other print materials?

Where can I locate suitable sources?

What content literacy strategies should I use?

This chapter also includes perspectives from two highly regarded authors: Joan Bauer and Will Hobbs.

Why Should I use Literature and Other Print Materials in My Content Classes?

A commonly held perception is that literature is almost exclusively the domain of the English language arts classroom and that history, science, math, and other courses of study are about specific facts, principles, and concepts. This limited view is detrimental to helping students develop broad contexts for their learning. Literature has the potential to put a human face on all learning, regardless of the content area. For example, students can read about the dumping of hazardous waste in a text chapter on the environment, but they gain an understanding of the human price of ecological disasters when reading James Lincoln Collier's *When the Stars Begin to Fall*. This book shows the power of industry, the economics of jobs held in the balance, the impact on the environment, and the dilemma the discovery of dumping causes for the protagonist. From a scientific perspective, it raises many environmental and ethical issues that can create lively class interaction. "Literature provides the context for understanding the significance of facts. In this way, students are able to transform knowledge into personally useful and meaningful tools for expanding their understanding of the world and themselves" (Siu-Runyan, 1995, p. 132).

Wilde (1998) describes the potential of supplementing the math text with literature: "Children's books are a rich resource for the applied areas of mathematics that get little attention in the curriculum. Geometry and measurement can involve more than textbook exercises if they are treated as ways of representing and understanding the world around us" (p. 129). Whitin and Wilde (1992) also speak to how both fiction and nonfiction can expand students' understanding of mathematics: "Children can learn to appreciate mathematics in ways that go far beyond computation: as a tool for solving real-life problems, a way of thinking and expressing knowledge, and a source of aesthetic pleasure and recreations" (p. 17).

Perhaps the connection between history and literature seems more obvious, because in some ways both are the stories of people, events, and recurring themes. Burke-Hengen (1995) discusses this connection and states that "Literature promotes empathy because of the ties that readers make between themselves and characters in stories and in history. I believe that when I encourage my students to find connections between their experiences, the thoughts and feelings that they have about them, and the experiences of people in books or in history, their understandings of events and ideas are more likely to be empathetic and more likely to be remembered and applied to new situations" (pp. 38–39).

Literature has a vital role to play in other disciplines, including the arts. Barbara Kiefer (1998) discusses the value of nonfiction books in helping children understand art:

> The best of these books will engage readers with the arts and deepen understandings of critical and historical perspectives. The books should involve children in the "how-to" of art making as well as the "why of a particular art form," and help them to make personal connections across time and across art forms. Whatever the format of the presentation or the author's purpose, books should give children information about the rich possibilities inherent in an aesthetic experience. (p. 147)

The high level of specialized knowledge in most content areas frequently contributes to the aridity of the texts and the distancing of students. Using literature in the content areas serves to heighten student involvement and interest and helps to create a personal sense of connection for students. Effective trade books are written by authors who combine a passion for content with skillful writing that connects with their readers. For example, students may read a textbook account of the Civil War that provides numerous statistics about injuries; however, Jim Murphy's *The Boys' War* presents much of the same information, but in a far more moving format.

Students connect with this book, in part, because they identify with the youth who fought on both sides. In this nonfiction book, Murphy (1990) provides a human context for the horrors of the Civil War.

> Suddenly, the war that had been a romantic dream was all around them like angry bees. Elisha Stockwell found himself facedown on the ground, shells exploding all around and soldiers screaming for help. "I want to say, as we lay there and the shells were flying over us, my thoughts went back to my home, and I thought a foolish boy I was to run away and get into such a mess as I was in. I would have been glad to have seen my father coming after me." (p. 33)

Teachers use literature in a variety of ways when teaching history, as suggested in the following scenario.

Terry Cass realized that his students would understand more about the American Revolution if he could humanize it for them. He read _The Fighting Ground_ by Avi to the class as an initiating experience to create interest in the Revolutionary War period. Each student then selected a novel about this period by either Ann Rinaldi or the Collier brothers to read and share in small groups.

♦ ♦ ♦

Fiction in a math class may seem like an unlikely curricular merger; however, Joan Bauer's book, *Sticks,* makes geometry and mathematical predictions come alive for students. As Whitin and Wilde (1992) point out, "Through books, learners see mathematics as a 'common human activity,' which can be used in various contexts" (p. 4). Bauer uses a pool competition as the springboard for teaching about angles and vectors. In the following section, award-winning author Joan Bauer talks about why she writes and what she hopes to accomplish in her work.

An Author's Perspective
JOAN BAUER

Joan Bauer was born in River Forest, Illinois, the eldest of three sisters. Her mother was a schoolteacher with a great comic sense; her father, a salesman that no one could say no to. Her maternal grandmother had been a famous storyteller and had a striking effect on Bauer's early years. "She would tell me stories with five different voices and as many dialects. I would sit on her enormous lap transfixed at how she could teach me about life and make me laugh through her stories. She taught me the significance of humor and how it intersects our daily lives."

Bauer managed an eclectic list of jobs from assistant typing teacher at age twelve to high school waitress. In her early twenties, she was a successful advertising and marketing salesperson. Professional writing for magazines and newspapers followed, then screenwriting, which was cut short by a serious car accident. She regrouped and wrote Squashed, *which won the Delacorte Prize for a First Young Adult Novel. Since then, she has written four more highly successful novels for young people and received other awards, including the Golden Kite.*

I very much want to write stories that have positive role models for young adults and show the connections between humor and pain. I'm trying to craft characters who are strong and make healthy decisions—people that I would like to know. I see a great deal of life personally through the lens of humor, so I naturally gravitate toward humor as a way to develop character and as a literary vehicle. I'm also interested in showing characters from different generations learning from each other. I think this is how life works, frankly. When we just spend time with people our own age, people who are exactly like us, there's a limited sphere from which we can learn and grow. Teenagers have a great deal to learn from their elders and vice versa. I also don't write stories about glamorous, popular people—I tend to look at the ordinary part of life (growing pumpkins, taking photographs, playing pool, selling shoes, loving history) and show how ordinary things can be made special. Few of us live charmed lives—I'm reminded of this every time I look in my messy closets.

I believe that my books can be used several ways in the classroom: thematically, to discuss issues facing young people today—as examples of how humor can discuss serious subjects; as a tool to show how to use laughter against the storms of life; as examples of how we learn from people of different ages. Strip away the humor in *Squashed* and you'll find a girl who has an extraordinary dream, a difficult relationship with her father, she is overweight, not popular, and her mother died in a car crash. This is a story about overcoming. Look beneath the laughter in *Thwonk* and see a teenager obsessed romantically with a boy who is wrong for her, and she will do just about anything to get him. *Thwonk* is about self-esteem—it is a warning not to judge people by their outward appearances; it redefines the notion of popularity. *Sticks* shows the pain of being bullied and how to fight back effectively. It explores how athletes overcome injuries and how skills are mastered. Its use is multi-disciplined since it incorporates math, science, and history into the plot. Mickey uses his knowledge of math and physics to win the pool tournament. At the core of *Rules of the Road* is a theme very important to me personally—great adversity, if we let it, can bring forth great growth and strength. Jenna Boller is inundated with problems—her alcoholic dad, her Alzheimer-stricken grandmother—but she refuses to let pain victimize her or define her. She rises above it and sees life through the lens of being an overcomer. She concentrates on what she's good at, she is kind in the face of unkindness, she doesn't let loss stop her. This is also a book that explores honor in business and the benefits of hard work. *Backwater* is a discourse on where we come from and how that defines us. It is a story of a girl who adores history and pulls from this love to help her understand the problems in her life. It also explores the vast differences in human personality, how to deal with difficult people, and how understanding others often streams from our acceptance of them as they are.

I found my humorous "voice" as a writer after I was in a serious car accident in 1987. I wasn't able to write for quite some time; I had extraordinary doubts if I would be able to write effectively again because of the nature of the injuries. I was so frightened. And in the midst of that, I got the idea to write a funny story about an overweight teenager who wanted to grow the biggest pumpkin in Iowa. That story was *Squashed* and the humor in it helped me get better. I laughed while I wrote it. I realized vividly how important laughter can be in the midst of pain. That is something I try to intersect throughout my work.

Selected Titles

Squashed	*Rules of the Road*
Thwonk	*Backwater*
Sticks	

The author of the *Magic School Bus* books, Joanna Cole, as quoted by Bamford and Kristo (1998), states: "It's better for a child to read one good science trade book than a whole textbook that teaches you that science is boring" (p. 240). Cerullo (1997) also describes the value of trade books for science: "Science trade books engage students' interest on both the intellectual and the emotional levels: this is why both fiction and nonfiction books belong in a science curriculum" (p. 1). Examples of highly effective wildlife and natural science trade books are the works of Dorothy Hinshaw Patent, such as *Biodiversity, Children Save the Rain Forest,* and *Eagles of America*. In *Habitats: Saving Wild Places*, she persuasively makes a case for balancing the protection of animals and plants with human needs. This book and ones like it help young people to weigh ethical issues such as the cost of progress in our society. Among the books naturalist and award-winning author Jean Craighead George writes are ecological mysteries, such as *The Missing' Gator of Gumbo Limbo* and *The Fire Bug Connection*, that engage students in pursuing environmental clues to solve crimes, but they must also wrestle with social issues and the consequences of progress.

Among the trade books that are applicable in virtually every discipline are biographies and autobiographies. The stories of those women and men who have made contributions to each field of study help to humanize a content area. For example, there are a number of simple biographies of famous artists which provide wonderful color reproductions of each artists' work as well as briefly telling their life stories. Kiefer (1998) describes their value: "One of the aims of nonfiction books on the arts should be to help children understand that an artist, musician, dancer, or poet is trying to convey profound human experiences and understandings in ways that cannot be expressed by words and sentences alone" (p. 145). Russell Freedman's award-winning biographies, such as *The Wright Brothers: How They Invented the Airplane, Lincoln: A Photobiography,* and *The Life and Death of Crazy Horse,* provide students not only with stories, but also with the distinctive flavor of the times and culture in which the individuals lived.

In addition to biographies, picture books are another genre that have wide application in the content areas. Bishop and Hickman (1992), while acknowledging that there are differing definitions of picture books, take a contemporary perspective: "... *picture books* include any book that appears in picture book format. ... Just about any definition of a picture book, however, includes the requirement that, in the marriage of words and pictures, the two partners share the responsibility of making the book work" (pp. 2–3). The recent trend in picture books is to appeal to a broad audience. These books intertwine content and illustrations that reflect events, issues, and social conditions and can be used in a range of content classes. Sometimes controversial, many of these picture books are definitely more appropriate for older readers than young children.

The follow scenarios describe how teachers use picture books in content classes.

In their unit on the Sixties in the social studies/English block, Erin O'Connor and Clark Henry provide the framework for their class to recognize and address the controversial nature of the Vietnam War. They use Eve Bunting's picture book, *The Wall,* to discuss the need for healing and the symbolic nature of the wall.

Carol Sparks introduced a science unit on the Rain Forest by using Judith Heide Gilliland's picture book, <u>River,</u> to initiate student interest and arouse curiosity. The richly colored illustrations provided the students with a visual context for the setting and created a frame of reference for them to understand the unique environment of the Rain Forest. They became familiar with the birds, animals, and vegetation and had a vivid image of the Amazon River to frame their study.

♦ ♦ ♦

Varied print materials can create student interest, helping them become active learners in a content area. Such sources also help students develop more complex, multi-layered understandings leading to richer, deeper conceptual learning of content. As Jeff Wilhelm (1998) asserts: "Nonfiction allows us to be ethnographers by observing and entering into other worlds and experiencing these places, people, and times that are often at a distance from us. Nonfiction also encourages us to imagine possibilities and ask 'What if?' and to be action researchers investigating how to enact changes in the world" (p. 218).

Using non-textbook print material effectively in the classroom is dependent upon establishing appropriate purposes for it. In the next section, we discuss what teachers should consider when they expand the reading boundaries of their students in content classes.

How do I Establish Appropriate Purposes for Using Literature and Other Print Materials?

The expansion of the curriculum to include literature and other materials is designed to make the classroom more responsive to the needs and interests of the students. Simply changing reading materials, however, is only the first step and by itself will not affect any significant change. Based on their research with using nonfiction trade books in content classrooms, Palmer and Stewart (1997) raise four issues:

1. The nature of assignments in content area classes may need to change in order to make full use of today's informational books with their in-depth coverage of topics.

2. Nonfiction [is] . . . sometimes . . . treated as another textbook or encyclopedia. . . . As a result, the rich potential for extended, meaningful reading of nonfiction trade books is lost.

3. Teachers and students require training in effective use of nonfiction trade books.

4. A proactive, knowledgeable librarian is essential when using nonfiction trade books in content area classes, and teachers should include the librarian in unit planning and implementation. (pp. 635–637)

Literature in the content classroom must complement and enhance the curriculum. Fiction and nonfiction must contribute to the students' ability to develop knowledge of the subject. Additionally, that knowledge must cumulatively contribute to the students' conceptual understanding of the content. The use of literature can produce a broad context for learning the multi-faceted nature of the content. As Palmer and Stewart note, however, using literature as if it were a textbook is counterproductive.

Figure 6.1 shows the framework for using literature in the content area classroom.

As more teachers use trade books in content classes, there is a trend by some authors of young adult fiction and children's fiction to write stories that have a significant informational component and more clearly defined classroom application. We have labeled these works *infofiction*.

Infofiction is fiction with an informational context that is, at times, as significant as the plot development and the evolution of characters. In this type of fiction, the plot is often dependent upon the "message" of the informational elements of the

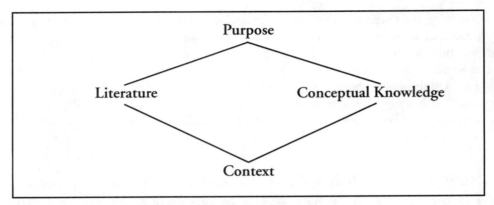

Figure 6.1 Literature Framework in the Content Classroom

work. For example, Joan Lowry Nixon's historical novels have significant historical information.

Infofiction is a merger of the narrative, made-up qualities of fiction with nonfiction informational perspectives. This merger or blending provides readers with books that, while primarily fictional, have factual information that helps them to develop a deeper level of content understanding.

Infofiction has certain characteristics that distinguish it from other types of fiction:

1. strong instructional connections with content areas other than English;

2. a theme in which factual information about a topic is explored;

3. the message of the information is as significant as the story.

Additionally, infofiction provides students with opportunities in which they can connect ideas with realistic, historical, or even futuristic situations and experience them vicariously. In the next section, Will Hobbs, who is a former teacher and a noted author of fiction that connects youthful readers with science and nature, discusses what he believes is important and what he hopes to achieve in his work.

An Author's Perspective
WILL HOBBS

Will Hobbs was born in Pittsburgh, Pennsylvania, but lived in many different places as a child due to his father's career in the Air Force. Will grew up mostly in Alaska, Texas, and California. He earned a B.A. and M.A. in English from Stanford University. Will and his wife live in southwestern Colorado, where his interests include reading, backpacking, whitewater rafting, archeology, anthropology, history, natural sciences, and gardening. And writing! For seventeen years he taught English and reading in the local schools, mostly at the middle school level. He's been a full-time writer since 1990.

Will Hobbs' books are widely used in the schools and have received numerous awards, including ALA Best Books for Young Adults, Notable Children's Trade Book in the Field of Social Studies, and Western Writers of America Spur Award.

With each new book, I set out to write fiction that has a page-turning quality, is character-based yet involves substantive content, and leaves the reader with a sense of hope and possibility. I hope to be writing about things that are important. Almost always, I portray a character struggling to become a better person. That's what it's all about.

My sense of audience comes from my years of teaching. It's gratifying to learn that my books appeal to readers all across the ability spectrum, from the most advanced to the reluctant. A boy from Michigan writes, "Before I read *Far North*, I didn't like to read much, but now I read quite often. I finally found books that interest me, and they're written by you." A letter like this one gives me goosebumps as a writer and as a former teacher.

I've found that if my story involves compelling characters in a compelling situation, I'm free to stretch as far as my interests and imagination will take me. In addition to my realistic novels, I've written a fantasy (*Kokopelli's Flute*) and a mystery (*Ghost Canoe*). In all of my books, I'm connecting kids with nature, usually a wild place I dearly love. I think of the

natural world as an endlessly renewable source of inspiration. After reading *Downriver* and *River Thunder*, which have a female protagonist, a girl from Virginia wrote, "I used to think that all the wonderful experiences nature has to offer had pretty much vanished from the face of the earth. Your books made me see that there are still some places that have been left to nature."

I'm a huge fan of independent reading—kids choosing their own titles—and I'm just as big a fan of *teaching* a novel as you read it aloud to the entire class. A dramatic oral reading allows kids to develop their inward ear for their own silent, independent reading. It's a tremendous compliment from classroom teachers when they tell me, "Your books make great read-alouds."

I often see my novels being taught across the curriculum, with the language arts teachers teaming with social studies and natural science teachers. Because novels are so emotional, they're a way to teach content in a way that will be remembered, because it touched the heart. *Kokopelli's Flute* becomes an invitation to further studies of archeology and the ancient

Americas, of native American folklore, of paleobotany and ethnobotany. The geography and the people of Canada are being taught in many schools in connection with *Far North.* Another example would be the wonderful units on endangered animals developed around *Changes in Latitudes* (sea turtles), *Bearstone* and *Beardance* (grizzly bears), and *The Maze* (California condors).

Books can be powerful trail signs in your life, pointing you in good directions and sometimes far from the beaten track. I hope my books will suggest to kids that it's still a wonderful world out there despite its terrible flaws. There's so much to explore, to get excited about, and it's very much in jeopardy. Everything depends on young people caring.

A teacher once pointed out to me that there's a line in one of my books that sums up "my message." I wondered what that line could possibly be. She said, "It's the last words of Johnny Raven, the elder in *Far North,* in his letter intended for the young people. Johnny's letter ended, 'Take care of the land, take care of yourself, take care of each other.'"

It only took a moment's reflection to realize that the teacher was right. In Johnny's message to the young people I had written my own.

Selected Titles

Changes in Latitudes	*Beardream*
Bearstone	*Ghost Canoe*
Downriver	*River Thunder*
The Big Wander	*Howling Hill*
Beardance	*The Maze*
Kokopelli's Flute	*Jason's Gold*
Far North	

As teachers develop appropriate purposes for using literature and other print materials in their classroom, they need access to a wide range of sources that are suitable for their content areas. In the next section, we describe how to locate these materials.

Where can I Locate Suitable Sources?

The decision to include literature and other print sources in content area classrooms depends on both the appropriate selection of books and determining an appropriate purpose for those books in the classroom. The issue of selection is complicated by the confusion or difficulty that content teachers have in identifying appropriate books that will be beneficial for their classes. One of their major concerns in using literature is where to locate appropriate materials for their students.

There are numerous resources available to assist teachers. Professional journals in many fields have articles about using trade books in their content areas. Additionally, a number of organizations have book lists of trade books that are particularly appropriate in their fields. Many publishers now divide their trade book catalogs by areas of interest that reflect content appropriateness.

Authors who write for young people explore widely varied topics in science, history, geography, math, the arts, music, and other areas. These topics are developed in fiction, nonfiction, and picture books. *VOYA (Voice of Youth Advocates)* has established an annual honor list of nonfiction "that librarians and teachers would and should consider for purchase. . . . a wide selection of excellent books . . . that are readable, interesting, and pertinent" (p. 162). The National Science Teachers Association also compiles an annual list of "Outstanding Science Trade Books for Children," in conjunction with the Children's Book Center. Their list is categorized by different scientific disciplines. The National Council for the Social Studies presents an annual listing of the Carter C. Woodson Award and Honor books. This award recognizes outstanding nonfiction in the field of social studies. Each year the National Council of Teachers of English identifies works of excellence in nonfiction. Their award, the *Orbis Pictus* Award, is presented to one recipient and to as many as five honor books. The selection committee also identifies other titles it considers to be outstanding. NCTE also annually selects thirty trade books that their selection committee determines to be Notable Children's Books. The International Reading Association annually presents the Children's Book Award in three categories: younger readers, older readers, and informational book. It also has an annual project, Teachers' Choices, to identify and publish information about books considered by teachers to be exceptional. Another project, conducted in conjunction with the Children's Book Council, identifies and publishes information about books voted as favorites by children and young adults across the country.

In addition to the varied book lists available, there are a number of sources for book reviews, including the following: *The ALAN Review,* a journal of the NCTE special interest group concerned with young adult literature. The center section of *The ALAN Review* includes "Clip and File Reviews" in an easy format for teachers to use. This journal also publishes articles on young adult literature and authors and regular columns addressing research, censorship, and other on-going concerns for educators.

Signal is the International Reading Association's journal of young adult literature. Its book review section includes recently published trade books that are recommended for young adults. The journal includes articles by and about authors, columns on multicultural literature, student surveys (listening to the voices of youths), reviews of professional resources, and information about books, authors, and conferences.

Other excellent sources of reviews are *Horn Book Magazine* and *The Horn Book Guide. Horn Book Magazine* is published six times a year and includes editorials, commentaries, articles—a number of which are written by authors of children's or young adult literature, reviews of recently published books with recommendations, and recommended books that have recently been published in paperback. The *Horn Book Guide*, published twice a year, is a critical annotated listing and rating of the trade books for children and young adults published each six months in the United States.

The New Advocate is published four times a year. It includes authoritative articles by or about authors who write for young people. These articles address a range of topics and genres. Additionally, columns address recently published trade books, professional resources, and children's responses to reading.

The Bulletin of the Center for Children's Books, published monthly, provides reviews of books with a coding system to guide readers. The journal includes an index by subject and use. Content area teachers can find useful resources by checking the index.

There are many lists of resources available to help facilitate teacher selection. In Appendix A, we provide the addresses of several professional organizations and journals. Appendix B lists current, major award-winning books.

Book Links from the American Library Association does an excellent job of providing insights for "teachers, librarians, library media specialists, booksellers, parents, and other adults interested in connecting children with books" (from the Mission Statement). The journal includes thematic bibliographies, articles by and about authors and illustrators, and regular departments. The bibliographies have interdisciplinary use.

Another major source of information about books and authors is the Internet. Most major publishers have web sites that feature information about new books. Many of the professional organizations also include information about their lists of suggested trade books on their web pages. There are also web sites that focus on literature and its place in the classroom. Numerous authors either maintain their own web pages or are the subject of web pages. Frequently, the greatest advantage to seeking information on the web is that many sites are linked to other related sites that may provide valuable information. Appendix C provides a listing of useful web sites.

As teachers locate suitable materials and develop appropriate purposes for its use, they also need to create meaningful learning experiences. In the next section, we describe how content literacy strategies can help teachers effectively use these materials.

What Content Literacy Strategies Should I Use?

Content literacy strategies help make a wide range of curricular materials more accessible for students. They also can help students construct meaning from what they are reading and utilize their understandings in meaningful ways. With the ever-increasing knowledge base of each content area, students need to learn ways in which they can make the necessary connections among concepts, ideas, and even broad subject areas. Content literacy strategies provide students with the means to make these types of connections. We believe that strategies for content literacy will help students to expand their knowledge and see content learning in broader contexts.

Additionally, connecting students through appropriate content literacy strategies with literature helps them to build personal learning that will enable them to become independent lifelong learners. Mary Burke-Hengen (1995) describes her own teaching experiences:

> Through our reading and the meanings that we construct because of it
> and the accompanying activities we engage in, we develop ideas that
> might otherwise seem abstract and unrelated, ideas like *freedom, war,
> choice, integrity,* and *victory*. Using literature in this way might be best
> described as the difference between asking middle-school students to

write an essay on an abstract topic of democracy and asking them to write a paper on the ways in which Sam Meeker lived his beliefs about government and what you think about his choice. The first format gives students little clue as to where to begin or how to give structure to their thoughts. In the second, there is a path to follow that is more likely to help students with their own particular thinking about an otherwise abstract subject. (p. 41)

We now turn our attention to strategies that will help teachers incorporate literature into their content classes.

Strategies for Literature in Content Classes

Initiating

The strategies in this section describe how literature can be used by content teachers to initiate topics, lesson, themes, or units.

STRATEGY: Teacher Read-Aloud

Component:	Content Literacy Process:	Organizing for Instruction:
Initiating Constructing Utilizing	Reading Writing Speaking Listening Viewing	Individual Pairs Small Group Whole Class

Description:

A teacher read-aloud has tremendous power to create interest and curiosity. Five minutes of an excerpt or an ongoing selection can effectively set the stage for important ideas and concepts. Teacher read-alouds are one of the easiest and most effective ways to initiate content topics.

Procedures:

- Materials for teacher read-alouds can be found almost anywhere. The major criteria for a selection beyond being pertinent and appropriate to the content and age group is length and writing style. Librarians can be of tremendous help in locating materials; newspapers, magazine, and journals are also useful sources.

- Teachers should quickly practice a selection before reading it to the class in order to know which words and phrases to emphasize. A teacher read-aloud can be greatly enhanced by varying tone and pitch to make the reading more dramatic.

- Prepare an introduction to the read-aloud to give the students a context for it. Follow-it up with a lead-in to the current topic.

Variations:

- Teachers also use read-alouds to interest students in independently reading books related to a particular topic or theme. They read a short excerpt that leaves the students wanting to know more and then say, "Anyone who wants to know what happens next may borrow this book from me."
- Teacher read-alouds can be effectively combined with many of the other initiating strategies described in Chapter 3.

Examples:

Michelle Martin began her class with a topic everyone was interested in: blood! "Where do blood cells come from?" she challenged her students. As she listed the students' hypotheses on the board, she asked another question: "Who was Florence Sabin and what does she have to do with our understanding of blood?" She then read to the class the excerpt, "The Dawn of Blood," from *Marvels of Science: 50 Fascinating 5-Minute Reads* by Kendall Haven.

To initiate a lesson on vocabulary during the geometry unit, Troy Pugalee read aloud *Sir Cumference and the First Round Table* by Cindy Neuschwander. The class found the story to be funny and it helped them understand and remember terms like radius, diameter, and circumference.

STRATEGY: From the Source

Component:	Content Literacy Process:	Organizing for Instruction:
Initiating Constructing Utilizing	Reading Writing Speaking Listening Viewing	Individual Pairs Small Group Whole Class

Description:

From the Source uses quotations to stimulate student interest and curiosity. Quotations, from literature and a wide range of other sources, serve as springboards to prompt students' questions and predictions. They also can help students to see connections between a content topic and events occurring today or in their own lives.

Procedures:

- Sources for quotations are many and varied, from traditional printed materials such as books, magazines, and journals to multi-media sources such as the Internet and CD-ROMs.
- The teacher displays the quotation on the board or overhead projector where everyone can see it.
- Then the teacher introduces it to the class, framing it within an appropriate context.
- Next, students respond to the quotation orally or in writing.
- The teacher uses their responses as a springboard for the current topic or lesson.

Variations:

- Students also can find quotations to present to the class.
- In classes where students write on a regular basis about the content topics, teachers may select (or have the students select) quotations from their own written work to use with this strategy.

Examples:

Christy Moore and Bob MacIntyre team teach an interdisciplinary social studies and language arts unit on the Holocaust. They used the following quote from *Lisa's War* (1987) by Carol Matas to get their students thinking about the role some teenagers played in the resistance movement.

> Suzanne has just killed a man. Shot in cold blood. Could I do the same? I think back to the mission she and I were on last week, with Stefan and an older man, Olaf. We blew up a shoe factory. About ten blocks from the blast, a German patrol car stopped us. (pp. 52–53)

Joel Farmington, science teacher, had the following quote from *Outward Dreams: Black Inventors and Their Inventions* (1991) by Jim Haskins written on the board when students entered the room. He had the students in small groups predict what they thought the device might be and what its impact was.

> Black inventors were making an impact upon American society that could hardly be ignored, and one such inventor, Jan Ernst Matzelinger (1852–1889), created a device that was so complex and advanced it could hardly be understood, let alone ignored. His invention affected everyone in their daily comings and goings, yet few knew his name or how he had improved their lives. (p. 36)

STRATEGY: Do You Know . . .?

Component:	Content Literacy Process:	Organizing for Instruction:
Initiating Constructing Utilizing	Reading Writing Speaking **Listening** Viewing	Individual Pairs Small Group **Whole Class**

Description:

Do You Know . . . ? is a quick strategy designed to pique students' curiosity on a specific topic. Well-focused or provocative questions create a tremendous need-to-know and help to dispel the air of passivity that students sometimes bring to a content area. The questions should not be general knowledge questions, easily answered questions, or review questions. Rather they should spark interest and create an air of excitement about the topic.

Procedures:

- The teacher asks a question or series of questions, using sentence stems such as "Do you know who . . . ?" or "Do you know why . . . ?" or ". . . when, where, what, or how . . . ?"
- The question is then followed-up by a teacher read-aloud or by having the students find and read a book that will help to answer the questions.

Variations:

- Students can use this same question format for presenting information they have read to the class.
- Some teachers have a learning center or bulletin board with Do you Know . . . ? questions accompanied by a collection of books or computer access for students.
- Students enjoy creating their own Do you know . . . ? questions.

Examples:

Darrin Graham frequently asked his students Do you know . . . ? questions based on information from sources such as *Ask Me Anything About The Presidents, 100 Events That Shaped World History*, and *1,0001 Things Everyone Should Know About American History*. Sometimes he reads the answers to the students, but other times he asks the questions just before they go to the library to guide their search for pertinent books.

Jennifer Lane's class was studying water pollution. She posed questions to them based on information in the book, *Environmental Experiments About Water* by Rybolt & Mebane. The students formulated hypotheses, conducted the experiments in the book, and then read other books that dealt with the effects of pollution such as the novel *Phoenix Rising* by Karen Hesse.

STRATEGY: Bridging

Component:	Content Literacy Process:	Organizing for Instruction:
Initiating	Reading	Individual
Constructing	Writing	Pairs
Utilizing	Speaking	Small Group
	Listening	Whole Class
	Viewing	

Description:

Students need assistance, at times, to develop sufficient prior knowledge before they encounter more difficult concepts or materials written at a more advanced level. Teachers use bridging with conceptually easier material to help students create an initial understanding and develop prior knowledge.

Procedures:

- The teacher has a range of classroom materials on any topic or unit.
- The teacher briefly introduces the materials to the class.
- Students select and read the material individually or in pairs.
- The teacher leads a discussion to help students build a framework to move to the new material.
- The teacher works with the class bridging between the previous material and the new.

Variation:

- While having a variety of reading materials is usually desirable, some teachers have everyone read the same bridging selection to help establish a common core of knowledge before moving on to more difficult material.

Example:

Martha Lane bridges young adult literature with the classics to encourage her students to read more widely. She uses *Tituba of Salem Village* by Ann Petry, *A Break with Charity* by Ann Rinaldi, and *In the Days of the Salem Witchcraft Trials* by Marilynne Roach to bridge with Arthur Miller's *The Crucible*.

STRATEGY: Picture Books

Component:	Content Literacy Process:	Organizing for Instruction:
Initiating	Reading	Individual
Constructing	Writing	Pairs
Utilizing	Speaking	Small Group
	Listening	Whole Class
	Viewing	

Description:

In this strategy, a teacher uses a picture book to initiate a specific topic or unit. Sometimes it is used to provide a common core of knowledge; other times it is used to provoke questions or stimulate interest and curiosity.

Procedures:

- The teacher selects an appropriate picture book for the topic or theme the class will be studying.
- The teacher begins by showing the book cover and asking students to speculate about what they will be learning.
- The teacher then reads the book aloud to the students.
- The teacher shows each illustration to the class, pausing to discuss what they are seeing.
- At the conclusion of the reading, the teacher uses the picture book as a springboard to the next topic or theme.

Variation:

- Some teachers have students find picture books to initiate the next topic or theme. In these cases, the teachers preview the picture books with the students and help them plan their class presentations.

Examples:

Layton Black uses Ken Mochizuki's *Baseball Saved Us*, a picture book about the Japanese Americans interred during World War II, as an introduction to this tragic, but largely unknown chapter in history. He follows up reading the picture book with excerpts from *A Fence Away from Freedom* by Ellen Levine, which recounts the experiences of young Japanese Americans in the camps.

Walker Chen reads Jean Craighead George's *Everglades* to his science students and shows them the paintings by Wendall Minor that illustrate it. In this way, the students are introduced to some information about this unique area and see what it is like at the same time.

Constructing

The strategies in this section describe how teachers can use literature during the constructing phase of the instructional framework to help students build rich, multi-layered conceptual understandings of content knowledge.

STRATEGY: The 5-Minute Book Talk

Component:	Content Literacy Process:	Organizing for Instruction:
Initiating	Reading	Individual
Constructing	Writing	Pairs
Utilizing	Speaking	Small Group
	Listening	Whole Class
	Viewing	

Description:

The 5-Minute Book Talk is an effective way for students to share what they read without the drudgery of the dreaded "book report." Listening to their peers talk about a book is also an excellent way to get other students interested in content-related literature. The 5-Minute Book Talks should be scheduled at regular intervals with no more than one or two at a time to keep interest high.

Procedures:

- Students select a book they want to read within the parameters established by the teacher.
- The teacher explains the guidelines for the 5-Minute Book Talk (see Figure 6.2) and students sign-up a 5-Minute Book Talk time.
- After each student gives a book talk, the other students write feedback (see Figure 6.3).

Variations:

- Many teachers find that graphic organizers (see Chapters 3 and 4 for descriptions) help students organize their book talks.

- Some teachers have their students create a visual representation to accompany their book talks.

- Book talks can be videotaped; they also can be written and sent via e-mail to a partner class or school.

- Some teachers give extra credit for a 5-Minute Book Talk whenever a student independently finds and reads a book related to something the class is studying.

Examples:

Dave Socia's class is doing a unit on the Civil War. With the aid of the librarian, he uses resource guides such as *Learning About . . . The Civil War: Literature and Other Resources for Young People* by Stephens and Brown to establish a large collection of books, both fiction and nonfiction at various reading levels, for the wide range of reading needs in his class. Students then select their books and sign up for 5-Minute Book Talks.

Student Moses Robertson wanted to know more about DNA after listening to the news accounts of the DNA testing conducted on the exhumed remains of the unknown soldier from the Vietnam War, who was buried in the Tomb of the Unknowns in Arlington National Cemetery. Moses gave a 5-Minute Book Talk on the book, *They Came from DNA*, part of the Scientific American Mysteries of Science series by Aronson.

Guidelines for 5-Minute Book Talk

1. Show your book to the class. Have the author's name, illustrator's name (if there is one), and the publication date written on the board or overhead projector.
2. Tell why you selected this book to read.
3. Describe 3 interesting parts of the book or 3 important things that you learned from reading it.
4. Make a recommendation: tell why you would or would not recommend that others in the class read it.

Figure 6.2

Feedback on 5-Minute Book Talk

1. Name of book and author; name of student giving book talk.
2. One or two things you remember about the book.
3. Something positive about the way the student gave the book talk.
4. Something the student might do differently next time.

Figure 6.3

STRATEGY: Memory Box

Component:	Content Literacy Process:	Organizing for Instruction:
Initiating	Reading	Individual
Constructing	Writing	Pairs
Utilizing	Speaking	Small Group
	Listening	Whole Class
	Viewing	

Description:

This strategy is used most effectively with fiction or biographies. Students identify key events in the lives of characters (real life figures or fictional ones) that they find particularly memorable. They represent each event with an object and collect the objects in a memory box.

Procedures:

- The teacher presents a book to the class by sharing a memory box that he or she has developed.
- As the class views each object, the teacher talks about its significance to the story or life of the character.
- Students select a novel or biography to read.
- They collect objects and prepare a memory box as they read.
- They share their memory boxes as a way of presenting their books to the class.

Variation:

- Some teachers have students write about the contents of their memory boxes rather than presenting them orally to the class.

Example:

Wayne Walters has each student in his general science class read a biography of a scientist and prepare a memory box about the figure's life to share with their fellow students.

STRATEGY: Explorer's Kit

Component:	Content Literacy Process:	Organizing for Instruction:
Initiating	Reading	Individual
Constructing	Writing	Pairs
Utilizing	Speaking	Small Group
	Listening	Whole Class
	Viewing	

Description:

In this strategy, students collect objects, symbols, and artifacts that they associate with what they are reading. The purpose of the collection is to help students interact with the content, construct meaning, and create a visual representation for the concepts, ideas, and issues.

Procedures:

- The teacher introduces a book about a topic the class is studying.
- The students are to think about the topic and the images it creates for them.
- The students then brainstorm on the board a list of objects that represent the topic.
- The teacher introduces the idea of an explorer's kits by showing one he or she has created.
- The students examine the objects that the teacher has identified.
- They compared their original list with objects from the kit.
- This activity serves as a foundation for students to develop their own kits on another topic.
- These kits will be presented to the class for discussion.

Variations:

- Some teachers give students lists of objects to locate as an initiating activity prior to reading a selection.
- Some teachers use the term Discovery Box in place of Explorer's Kit.

Example:

Lisa Erickson has numerous fossils and several informational books on that topic in her science class. She has students in their exploring groups put together an explorer's kit, listing and collecting equipment for an exploration (magnifying glasses, brushes, and other necessary tools). Then they embark on an expedition in the classroom to find fossils and related materials for their study.

STRATEGY: Dialogue Journals

Component:	Content Literacy Process:	Organizing for Instruction:
Initiating	Reading	Individual
Constructing	Writing	Pairs
Utilizing	Speaking	Small Group
	Listening	Whole Class
	Viewing	

Description:

A dialogue journal is designed to give students an opportunity to apply the knowledge they have constructed through a written dialogue with another student. The dialogue journal is where two or more students have the opportunity to "talk" with each other about their reactions, thoughts, and beliefs about a particular theme, concept, or idea. Students write a focused response in which they respond to specific ideas rather than summarizing the whole book. They share these responses with their learning partner or another group member who then writes a reaction to the original.

Procedures:

- The teacher begins the dialogue journal by having students select one entry from the journal where they write reactions to their reading and to class discussions.
- The students submit the entry and the teacher models the type of thoughtful responses that they will use in the dialogue journals.
- Upon returning the entries to the students, the teacher conducts a class discussion to determine appropriate responses.
- The teacher and students determine the appropriate length for responses. For example, in most cases responses should be from 4 to 6 complete sentences.
- Students complete a journal entry of half to three quarters of a page, either in or out of class.
- Students exchange their entries and write responses to what each other has written.
- The response process should not take more than ten to fifteen minutes.
- Students may then respond to the comments of their learning partners.

Variations:

- Some teachers use the dialogue process to interact with students themselves. The difficulty with this is, of course, the tremendous amount of time it takes to respond, meaningfully, to each student.

- Sometimes dialogue journal are used between classes. For example, two sections of American history might exchange their journals.

Example:

Mary Ellen Rogers uses dialogue journals to help her students express their reactions to a novel they are reading about AIDs. Paula Fox's *Eagle Kites* provokes strong reactions from students. Dialogue journals exchanged between student pairs give them an opportunity to express differing responses to it.

STRATEGY: VIP Maps

Component:	Content Literacy Process:	Organizing for Instruction:
Initiating	Reading	Individual
Constructing	Writing	Pairs
Utilizing	Speaking	Small Group
	Listening	Whole Class
	Viewing	

Description:

This mapping strategy (Stephens & Brown, 1998) is designed to engage students with an in-depth knowledge of the events or circumstances in the life of a significant figure. The strategy is used when students are reading an autobiography, biography, or lengthy biographical profile of the individual. By using a mapping approach for this strategy, students develop a graphic representation of the person's life that helps them develop a deeper understanding of the individual.

Procedures:

- The teacher models how to create a VIP map (see Figure 6.4) and discusses what information should go in each category.
- Students read material about an individual.
- They look for key information as they read, using the VIP map as a guide.
- Students begin to fill out the map, doing the sections "growing up," "personal characteristics," "major events," and "major contributions," as they read.
- The last two categories: "my reactions," and "I want to know more about . . ." are reflective ones that students do after completing their reading.
- VIP maps can be used for individual presentations, class discussion, or as a springboard for writing. They can also be displayed in the classroom or put in content notebooks or portfolios.

Variation:

- The VIP map can be used as an individual or group listening strategy when the teacher uses a read-aloud.

Example:

In music appreciation, Matt Peters has his students read a biography of a classical composer. Students develop a VIP map on their composer and prepare a class presentation. The presentation begins with the students playing a 2–4 minute selection of the composer's work. Each student then presents a VIP Map and talks about the composer's life and works.

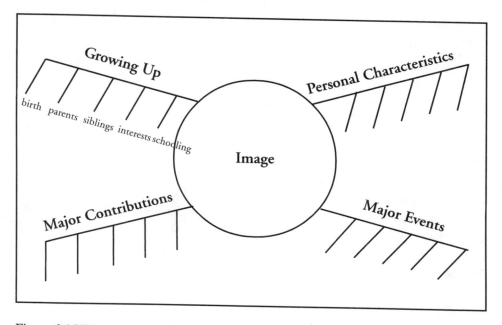

Figure 6.4 VIP Map (Stephens & Brown, 1998, pp. 9–10)

STRATEGY: Values Mapping

Component:	Content Literacy Process:	Organizing for Instruction:
Initiating	Reading	Individual
Constructing	Writing	Pairs
Utilizing	Speaking	Small Group
	Listening	Whole Class
	Viewing	

Description:

This strategy is designed to help students recognize the values inherent in the fiction they are reading that influence decision-making, social issues, and environmental issues, among others. The process is for students to identify a value that is significantly explored in the work and then find evidence that supports it.

Procedures:

- Together the teacher and class identify a list of the values from a novel they have read.
- Individually students select a value they believe plays a significant role in the book as well as in American society.
- Students find evidence for the value in the novel.
- The students map their findings by placing the value in a circle in the center of their paper.
- Then they connect to the value citations of evidence (see Figure 6.5).

Variation:

- Some teachers have their students use direct quotes from the book for evidence, while others have students paraphrase them.

Examples:

Tom Blake had his students read David Klass' *California Blue* and identify ecological issues and map the values associated with them.

Joyce Hansen's historical novels *Which Way Freedom?* and *Out From This Place* deal with the Civil War period. Lynne Ramsey's students each choose to read one of the books. They then select a value that they think is important in the story and find quotes as evidence of its significance.

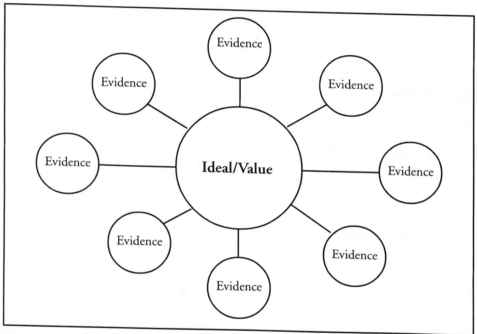

Figure 6.5 Values Map

(From *Teaching Young Adult Literature: Sharing the Connection* by Jean E. Brown and Elaine C. Stephens, Wadsworth Publishing, 1995)

STRATEGY: Infofiction

Component:	Content Literacy Process:	Organizing for Instruction:
Initiating Constructing Utilizing	Reading Writing Speaking Listening Viewing	Individual Pairs Small Group Whole Class

Description:

In this strategy, students read novels that have a significant informational dimension. As students read novels that combine fact with fiction (see explanation of infofiction on p. 167–168), teachers help them to identify the principles or concepts that are presented factually. Recognizing verifiable factual information in their reading of fiction provides students with a foundation to make connections between their content learning and the novel. Students record the informational content of the book on a chart as they read. These charts are then used as springboards for verification of the information and for further investigation about the topic. Their charts can also be used as springboards for writing about the book.

Procedures:

- The teacher models searching for informational content in fiction.
- The teacher provides students with a display of a number of novels that contain significant informational content, e. g., Will Hobbs' *Kokopelli's Flute*.
- Students select a book from the teacher's recommended list or classroom library display.
- While reading the novel, students identify the informational content in the book.
- Students then create a chart of the information (see Figure 6.6) that they have found.
- Students verify the information.
- Students, along with their teachers, plan further investigation of the information and its implications.
- Teachers plan follow-up writing activities or other experiences where the students use the information.

Variations:

- Some teachers have their students report their findings orally to the class.
- Some teachers have students reflect on the book by determining what contribution the factual content made to the story.

Example:

The following chart presents one approach to having students record factual content.

Book Title and Author		
Factual Information	Page #	Verification Source

Figure 6.6 Infofiction Chart

Strategies (cont.)

STRATEGY: Investigative Teams

Component:	Content Literacy Process:	Organizing for Instruction:
Initiating	Reading	Individual
Constructing	Writing	Pairs
Utilizing	Speaking	Small Group
	Listening	Whole Class
	Viewing	

Description:

Investigative Teams is a strategy designed to provide a structure and format for reading and discussing content-related literature in small groups. We created it in response to the needs of teachers who liked using literature circles (Daniels, 1994), but found that those particular discussion roles did not lend themselves well to either nonfiction or the informational content of infofiction. Investigative Teams is based upon the concept of a newspaper; the discussion roles are structured to reflect the duties and responsibilities of people who work on a newspaper. Using this strategy, students select books, form small groups based on the books, and then assume specific roles as their basis for responding and discussing the book.

Investigative Team Roles:

There are nine Investigative Team roles: investigative reporter, headline writer, graphic artist, editorial consultant, critic, travel reporter, ad designer, researcher, and social columnist. The following section provides descriptions and directions to the students. Information for each role should be on a separate sheet when given to the students.

Procedures:

- The teacher establishes a limited collection of books related to a topic or theme. In a typical class, this limited collection might consist of 3–7 different titles, with enough copies of each title for small groups (teams) of 4 or 5 students. In some situations, the whole class may be reading the same book.
- The teacher reviews the 9 roles (see ps. 198–206.) and selects those that fit the particular content area, the topic or theme, and the collection of books. Usually 4 or 5 different roles are selected, but the investigative reporter is always one of the roles because this individual initiates the discussion.

- The teacher introduces the selected roles to the class and uses short selections to provide practice with how to respond using each role.
- The students then select their books and form groups called Investigative Teams. All the students in a team will be reading the same book.
- Each student in the group chooses a different role. Students know that as they read and discuss the book, they will rotate roles. Generally everyone in the Investigative Team will have a turn with each role.
- The teacher and class establish a calendar for reading and responding, for meeting in their groups for discussion, and for rotating roles.
- Students read the first part of their books and prepare for the Investigative Team discussion by responding to the appropriate role sheet.
- Investigative Teams meet and discuss the first part of the book with the team members responding based on their role. The goal is for the discussion to be interactive rather than conducted with a "taking-turns" format. The role sheets ensure that students have prepared for the discussion and bring several different perspectives to it.
- At the conclusion of the each Investigative Team meeting, students assess the discussion, rotate roles, and make preliminary plans for the next meeting.

Variation:

- Frequently teachers begin Investigative Teams by having everyone read the same book to help the class learn the roles and procedures. Student choice, however, is an essential ingredient in the successful use of content-related literature. There should also be opportunities for students to form groups based on selecting different books.

Examples:

Nancy VanderMyer used Investigative Teams with nonfiction about the Civil War. The students chose books and formed groups using the following titles: *For Home and Country: A Civil War Scrapbook* by Bolotin and Herb; *A Separate Battle: Women and the Civil War* by Chang; *The Boys' War: Confederate and Union Soldiers Talk About the Civil War* by Murphy; *Behind the Blue and Gray: The Soldier's Life in the Civil War* by Ray; and *Behind the Lines: A Sourcebook on the Civil War* by Smith. All of the groups used the following roles: investigative reporter, headline writer, graphic artist, and the critic. Depending upon the book, some groups also used the role of social columnist or travel reporter.

Kerry Green used Investigative Teams with two science fiction novels to explore the social consequences of scientific advances. Students chose to read either *Invitation to the Game* by Monica Hughes or *Fahrenheit 451* by Ray Bradbury. The Investigative Teams used the following roles: investigative reporter, headline writer, editorial consultant, and social columnist.

INVESTIGATIVE REPORTER

Your Name: _____   Date: _____

Selection: _____

As the investigative reporter, you are responsible for asking questions about the selection that get the other members of the group talking about what they read. You should get the group started with a question that will make everyone think. Then let everyone else have a turn to talk. It is *not* your job to tell people that they are right or wrong, but to get them thinking and talking. You *can* ask them to explain their answers and show their evidence from the selection.

Possible thinking questions:

1. _____

   _____

2. _____

   _____

3. _____

   _____

4. _____

   _____

5. _____

   _____

HEADLINE WRITER

Your Name: _____   Date: _____

Selection: _____

As the headline writer, your job is to read the selection and then create several possible headlines that reflect its content and also grab the readers' attention. Present your headlines to the group and have them discuss what they think of each one.

Possible headlines

1. _____

2. _____

3. _____

GRAPHIC ARTIST

Your Name: _____   Date: _____

Selection: _____

As the graphic artist, your job is to read the selection and then create a visual inter-pretation of it. It should make the readers react to the selection. You might draw a picture or a cartoon or make a collage. Or you might find a picture or photograph made by someone else. Present your visual to the group and get them discussing what they think it means.

Brainstorm ideas for a visual interpretation of the selection:
(Put your visual on the back of this sheet or another piece of paper.)

EDITORIAL CONSULTANT

Your Name: _____   Date: _____

Selection: _____

As the editorial consultant, your job is to help the group make connections between the selection and things that are happening now. You might consider why the information in the selection is important for us to know or how we can use the information in our lives. You might also make connections between the selection and current events, issues, or people.

Possible connections:

1. _____

   _____

2. _____

   _____

3. _____

   _____

4. _____

   _____

5. _____

   _____

THE CRITIC

Your Name: _____   Date: _____

Selection: _____

As the critic, your job is to help the group discuss their personal reactions to the selection and to critique it. You might ask them questions about what they liked and disliked about it or what they thought were the strong and weak points of the selection. You might also have them discuss the writing style and whether it held their interest or not.

Possible critic's questions:

1. _____

   _____

2. _____

   _____

3. _____

   _____

4. _____

   _____

5. _____

   _____

TRAVEL REPORTER

Your Name: _____   Date: _____

Selection: _____

As the travel reporter, your job is to help the group understand information in the selection related to maps, traveling conditions, and specific geographical locations. You should also help the group understand the time frame of the events in the selection.

Important travel and time information:

AD DESIGNER

Your Name: _____   Date: _____

Selection: _____

As the ad designer, your job is to read the selection and then design an ad for a product connected with it. The product could be an actual object or something imaginary that you create. Present your ad to the group and get them discussing how it relates to the selection.

Brainstorm ideas for an ad related to the selection:
(Put your ad on the back of this sheet or another piece of paper.)

RESEARCHER

Your Name: _____   Date: _____

Selection: _____

As the researcher, your job is to locate other reading selections that relate to this selection and present them to the group. You might find other types of reading materials. Or you might find other topics related to the topic in this selection.

Possible related readings:

1. _____

2. _____

3. _____

4. _____

5. _____

SOCIAL COLUMNIST

Your Name: _____   Date: _____

Selection: _____

As the social columnist, your job is help the group explore the social conditions of the time period in which the selection is set. You might discuss what daily life was like for different groups of people. You might also discuss common beliefs, accepted roles, prejudices, and other examples of how people thought and felt during this time.

Possible social questions:

1. _____

   _____

2. _____

   _____

3. _____

   _____

4. _____

   _____

5. _____

   _____

Utilizing

This section describes strategies that can be used with literature during the utilizing phase of the instructional framework.

STRATEGY: Create a Talisman

Component:	Content Literacy Process:	Organizing for Instruction:
Initiating	Reading	Individual
Constructing	Writing	Pairs
Utilizing	Speaking	Small Group
	Listening	Whole Class
	Viewing	

Description:

Create a Talisman (Brown and Stephens, 1998) is a strategy designed to heighten student involvement with a major character from their reading. It can be used with fiction, biographies/autobiographies, and some nonfiction. When using this strategy, the reader selects a specific character for intensive study, culminating in identifying, creating, or designing a talisman for that character. A talisman is an object or charm thought to avert evil and bring about good fortune. In order to select an appropriate talisman, the reader must have a well-developed understanding of the character. The talisman may be either a concrete object or an abstract one. The object chosen to be the talisman should be one that the character does not possess.

Procedures:

- Students select a character from a book they've read.
- Students analyze the character by responding to the questions such as the following:

  What is the character like?

  What motivates him or her?

  How is the character viewed by other characters?

  Identify key words that give insights into the character.

  What objects remind you of the character? Why?

  Are there objects that you think represent aspects of the character? What and why?

Close your eyes and visualize the character. Jot down characteristics that you think the character has. If you were to visualize an object that reminds you of the character, what might it be?

- Students analyze the cultural heritage of the character by responding to questions such as the following:

  What customs, traditions, rituals, or symbols of the culture have played a role in the character's life?

  What is their impact on the character?

  How does this heritage influence his or her actions and behavior?

- Having gained insights about the characters and culture from which they come from, students design a talisman for the character.

Variation:

Students may choose to create a talisman for an author after they have read several of his or her books or in preparation for an author visit.

Examples:

One of Patrick McBride's students brought a shark's tooth to school as a talisman for Sonny from Graham Salisbury's *Blue Skin of the Sea*. The shark's tooth represented Sonny's struggle to overcome his fear of the ocean.

William Golden's students read Marion Dane Bauer's novel, *Face to Face,* and created a class mural that symbolized the internal and external obstacles that Michael faced. Each student pair incorporated a talisman for Michael within the design of the mural.

STRATEGY: Character Home Pages

Component:	Content Literacy Process:	Organizing for Instruction:
Initiating	Reading	Individual
Constructing	Writing	Pairs
Utilizing	Speaking	Small Group
	Listening	Whole Class
	Viewing	

Description:

This strategy is designed to capitalize on student interest in technology and in "surfing the net." Students create a "home page" for a character that they have selected from their reading. Their selection should be a major character that they know a great deal about because they will write the home page from the perspective of that character.

Procedures:

- The teacher models developing a home page for a character from a book that the whole class has read.
- Students identify an individual character that they wish to study in-depth.
- Students assume the point of view of the character.
- Students design a home page about the character that includes the following basic information:

  Personal information:
  age
  family
  school
  friends
  Characteristics:
  "What I look like . . ."
  "What I am like . . ."
  Interests and hobbies:

Variations:

- Some teachers use this strategy to have their students explore other aspects of a book—for example, the setting.
- This strategy can also be used with historical figures or biographical subjects.
- Some teachers use a thematic approach to web pages. They have their students explore a theme such as survival. In a case like this, students may use several books and the experiences of a number of characters as they struggle to survive.

Examples:

Nelson Gordon's history class is involved in a unit called the "Revolutionary War Alive." All of his students read a biography of a figure from the period. Students create a web page for the subject of the biography they have read. He finds that using a medium of the 1990s to present figures from over 200 years ago makes the historical figures less remote and his students are more receptive to learning about the period than have been previously.

Dee Charles has her students draw a detailed map of the town in Gary Paulsen's *The Monument*. She then has them create a home page for the town.

STRATEGY: People Portraits

Component:	Content Literacy Process:	Organizing for Instruction:
Initiating	Reading	Individual
Constructing	Writing	Pairs
Utilizing	Speaking	Small Group
	Listening	Whole Class
	Viewing	

Description:

This strategy is designed to help students focus on the changes and developments that people undergo. The strategy can be used with both fiction and nonfiction. Students, in groups, examine the appearance, personality, and the actions of the person at various points in the book.

Procedures:

- The teacher provides every student with a chart (see Figure 6.7) that is divided into thirds, representing the first third of the book, the second third, and the final third.
- The class is divided into three groups. Group 1 focuses on the first third of the book; group 2, the middle third; and group 3, the final third.
- Each group focuses on the evolution of the subject of the book by describing his or her appearance, personality, and actions in the third of the book that they have been assigned.
- As a group, students complete the chart for their section of the book.
- Each group reports to the class.
- The class then discusses the growth and changes in the person.

Variation:

Some teachers vary the categories that they have students respond to, for example, the person's accomplishments.

Example:

People Portrait Chart

Person	Appearance	Actions	Personality
1st third			
2nd third			
3rd third			

Figure 6.7

STRATEGY: Author Home Pages

Component:	Content Literacy Process:	Organizing for Instruction:
Initiating	Reading	Individual
Constructing	Writing	Pairs
Utilizing	Speaking	Small Group
	Listening	Whole Class
	Viewing	

Description:

This strategy is designed to capitalize on student interest in technology and in "surfing the net" by having them create a "home page" for an author whose work they particularly enjoy. Students should be familiar with several of the author's works. They will write the home page to provide background information about the author and the works.

Procedures:

- The teacher models developing a home page for an author, preferably one whose work the whole class has read.
- Students identify an author that they wish to study in-depth.
- The teacher has the class brainstorm the elements (see Figure 6.8) that they will include on their author's page.
- Students use the elements as a guideline for collecting materials and information.
- They then design and compose the author's pages.

Variation:

- Some students conduct e-mail interviews with the author as another source of information for the author home page they are creating.

Example:

Elements for Author's Page
Biographical Information
List of Books
Summary of Selected Books
Author's Comments about Books (when available)
Awards
Recommendations—from students or from critics

Figure 6.8

STRATEGY: Clues for You

Component:	Content Literacy Process:	Organizing for Instruction:
Initiating	Reading	Individual
Constructing	Writing	Pairs
Utilizing	Speaking	Small Group
	Listening	Whole Class
	Viewing	

Description:

In this strategy, students have the opportunity for two types of involvement with their reading. The first experience is to create a set of clues about a book or an author. The second experience is to examine a box or bag of clues created by another member of the class.

Procedures:

- The teacher shows several examples of Clue Boxes or Clue Bags, modeling for students how to create their own.
- Students begin by selecting either a book or author that they want to encourage their classmates to experience.
- They then create an "Invitation Card," composed of a picture, graphic, or an intriguing phrase or description that doesn't specifically reveal either the author or the book title. These cards are crucial to getting the attention of prospective readers.
- The Invitation Card will be attached to the outside of the Clue Boxes or Bags.
- As the students read, they develop a series of clue cards (from 7–10 cards) which they place in either a Clue Box or Bag.
- Once the clues are all collected, the Clue Box or Bag will be ready for examination.
- The completed Clue Boxes or Bags are displayed where other students may select them.
- As students examine each clue, they record on a pad of paper what they think it represents. Then, based on the clues, they guess the author or book title.
- The purpose of Clues for You is to get students interested in reading, not to produce winners and losers.

Variation:

- Some teachers let students also use objects as their clues.

Example:

Ann Albright has a number of illustrated biographies of artists and their work. She has her students check one out, read it, and then develop a set of clues focusing on characteristics of the artist's work.

STRATEGY: Across The Years

Component:	Content Literacy Process:	Organizing for Instruction:
Initiating	Reading	Individual
Constructing	Writing	Pairs
Utilizing	Speaking	Small Group
	Listening	Whole Class
	Viewing	

Description:

This strategy is modeled after the old PBS show, *Meeting of the Minds,* in which Steve Allen brought notable figures from different fields and from different time periods together to share ideas. Students research figures who have played a significant role in the development of a discipline, e. g. science. They then role play the figures by presenting their ideas and perspectives. They demonstrate how ideas have changed over the years.

Procedures:

- The teacher models assuming the role of a pioneer in the field, e. g., Madame Curie, Sir Francis Drake, Charles Darwin, Jane Austin, or Margaret Meade.
- The teacher identifies a number of other significant figures from different periods.
- The teacher has the class brainstorm the types of information that they would like to learn from the figures.
- Students, individually or in small groups, select a figure and research the person.
- They then prepare a presentation in which one member of each group will assume the role of the figure in order to discuss his or her contributions and accomplishments.

Variations:

- In more advanced classes, actual dialogues among figures from different times may be used as a follow-up to the initial presentation.
- In some classes, students dress in the role they are playing and have props from the time when the person lived. In this way, the students present a total sense of the period that their figure is from.
- In middle schools where interdisciplinary courses and team teaching are being used, students may select figures from a number of different academic areas.

Example:

In his economics class, Gordon Thompson has students assume the roles of Thomas Jefferson, Abraham Lincoln, Herbert Hoover, Lyndon Johnson, and Bill Clinton to present the economic conditions that they faced during their presidency. They then discussed the economic actions and policies that they enacted.

STRATEGY: Creating Content-Related Picture Books

Component:	Content Literacy Process:	Organizing for Instruction:
Initiating	Reading	Individual
Constructing	Writing	Pairs
Utilizing	Speaking	Small Group
	Listening	Whole Class
	Viewing	

Description:

Creating picture books, with text and illustrations equally providing the information, is an effective way for students to apply the concepts they have learned in a content class. Writing and illustrating content-related picture books can be done individually, in pairs, or in small groups, but there should be ample opportunities to share the finished books with others.

Procedures:

- The teacher shares a number of a content-related picture books with the class.
- Together they develop a model to follow for creating their own content-related picture book.
- A topic is selected, information is brainstormed, and any additional research is conducted.
- A storyboard is created, sketching out the format and basic content for the book.
- Then the text for the book is drafted.
- Pictures and illustrations are created or obtained.
- The text is revised and edited.
- The text is illustrated.
- The completed picture book is presented to the class.

Variation:

- Large collections of clip art or computer scanned illustrations may help students who are not comfortable with their artistic skills. Teachers need to be aware of copyright rules for whatever is used.

Examples:

In Kevin Carter's health classes, students created picture books on the effects of smoking.

In Mary Warren's French classes, students explored different regions of France in books and on the Internet. Then in small groups they wrote and illustrated picture book travelogues.

STRATEGY: Honoring Excellence In . . .

Component:	Content Literacy Process:	Organizing for Instruction:
Initiating	Reading	Individual
Constructing	Writing	Pairs
Utilizing	Speaking	Small Group
	Listening	Whole Class
	Viewing	

Description:

This strategy is designed to give readers the opportunity to honor books that they have enjoyed by creating an award category. To create this category, students read and discuss books that share a common element, theme, or genre (for example, strong female protagonists, survival books, or fantasy series). Students also establish criteria for recognizing the book(s) and assessing their literary merit. An effective feature of this strategy is that it can be structured to accommodate a wide range of student reading levels and backgrounds. According to their reading experiences, students may be able to complete the strategy with a learning partner, in small groups, or as a whole class. Regardless of the grouping pattern, the sharing of titles and information about books contributes to a lively class discussion.

Procedures:

- The initial step is for students to create or identify a broad category for the award. For example, students select a genre such as science fiction or a topic such as sports fiction.
- Students determine the conditions or limits of the award.
- Next, they create a name for the award that indicates what they are honoring.
- Students, then, identify criteria for selecting books. The criteria should also address issues of literary merit.
- Students must read widely in the field for which they will give the award, measuring each book against the criteria.
- Finally, students identify the primary recipient for their award and from one to three runners-up or honor books.
- Students then present their award and the recipient lists to the class.

Variation:

- Advanced students may choose to do their own awards individually, rather than in small groups or with a learning partner.

Example:

When using this strategy, Harriet Harvey schedules an Award Banquet as the culminating activity for all her social studies students. They meet in the school cafeteria for a special buffet supplied by parents. She provides all the students with a printed program that has their awards and its nominees listed. Each group presents its category for the award, its nominees, and its winner. One designated group member (the recipient) receives an award certificate for the winning entry. The recipient wears a costume that is appropriate for the category. For example, one group chose to honor the best novels of the Civil War period and they called their award, "The Blue and the Grey." The nominees were *Red Cap* by Clifton Wisler, Joan Nixon Lowrey's *A Dangerous Promise*, William O. Steele's *The Perilous Road*, and *With Every Drop of Blood* by Christopher and James Lincoln Collier. When *With Every Drop of Blood* was announced as the winner, two recipients—one in a Union uniform and one in a Confederate uniform—accepted the honor.

Literature Cited

Aronson, B. (1993). *They came from DNA*. New York: W. H. Freeman.

Avi (1984). *The fighting ground*. New York: HarperTrophy.

Bauer, J. (1996). *Sticks*. New York: Delacorte Press.

Bauer, M. D. (1991). *Face to Face*. New York: Clarion Books.

Bolotin, N., & Herb, A. (1995). *For home and country: A Civil War scrapbook*. New York: Lodestar Books.

Bradbury, R. (1953). *Fahrenheit 451*. New York: Ballantine.

Bunting, E. (1990). *The wall*. Illus. by Ronald Himler. New York: Clarion Books.

Chang, I. (1991). *A separate battle: Women and the Civil War*. New York: Lodestar Books.

Collier, J. L. (1986). *When the stars begin to fall*. New York: Bantam, Doubleday Dell Publishing.

Collier, J. L. & Collier, C. (1994). *With every drop of blood*. New York: Delacorte.

Fox, P. (1995). *The eagle kite*. New York: Orchard Books.

Freedman, R. (1996). *The life and death of crazy horse*. New York: Scholastic.

Freedman, R. (1987). *Lincoln: A photobiography*. New York: Scholastic.

Freedman, R. (1991). *The Wright brothers: How they invented the airplane*. New York: Holiday House.

Garraty, J. (1989). *1,001 things everyone should know about american history*. New York: Doubleday.

George, J. C. (1995). *Everglades*. Illus. by W. Minor. New York: HarperCollins.

George, J. C. (1993). *The fire bug connection*. New York: HarperTrophy.

George, J. C. (1993). *The missing 'gator of Gumbo Grove*. New York: HarperTrophy.

George, J. C. (1971, 1991). *Who really killed cock robin?* New York: HarperTrophy.

Gilliland, J. H., (1993). *River*. illus. by Joyce Powzyk. New York: Clarion Press.

Hansen, J. (1988). *Out from this place*. New York: Avon Books.

Hansen, J. (1986). *Which way freedom?* New York: Avon Books.

Haskins, J. (1991). *Outward dreams: Black inventors and their inventions*. New York: Bantam Books

Haven, K. (1994). *Marvels of science: 50 fascinating 5-minute reads*. Englewood, CO: Libraries Unlimited, Inc.

Hesse, K. (1994). *Phoenix rising*. New York: Puffin Books.

Hobbs, W. (1995). *Kokopelli's flute*. New York: Atheneum Books.

Hughes, M. (1990). *Invitation to the game*. Toronto, On.: HarperCollins.

Klass, D. (1994). *California blue*. New York: Scholastic.

Levine, E. (1995). *A fence away from freedom*. New York: G.P. Putnam's Sons.

Lowrey, J. N. (1994). *A dangerous promise*. New York: Bantam Doubleday Dell.

Matas, C. (1987). *Lisa's war*. New York: Scholastic

Miller, A. (1995). *The crucible: A play in four acts*. New York: Penguin Edition.

Mochizuki, K. (1993). *Baseball saved us*. New York: Lee & Low.

Murphy, J. (1990). *The boys' war: Confederate and union soldiers talk about the civil war*. New York: Clarion Books.

Neuschwander, C. (1988). *Sir Cumference and the First Round Table*. Illus. by W. Geehan. New York: Charlesbridge Publishers.

Patent, D. H. (1993). *Habitats saving wild places.* Hillside, NJ: Enslow Publishers.

Paulsen, G. (1991). *The monument.* New York: Delacorte Press.

Petry, A. (1964). *Tituba of Salem Village.* New York: HarperCollins.

Phillips, L. (1992). *Ask me anything about the presidents.* New York: Avon Books.

Ray, D. (1991). *Behind the Blue and Gray: The soldier's life in the Civil War.* New York: Scholastic Press.

Rinaldi, A. (1992). *A break with charity.* Orlando, FL: Harcourt Brace Jovanovich.

Roach, M. K. (1996). *In the days of the Salem witchcraft trials.* New York: Houghton Mifflin Company.

Rybolt, T. R. & Mebane, R. C. (1993). *Environmental experiments about water.* Hillside, NJ: Enslow.

Salisbury, G. (1992). *Blue skin of the sea.* New York: Delacorte.

Smith, C. (1993). *Behind the lines: A sourcebook on the Civil War.* New York: Millbrook Press.

Steele, W. O. (1958, 1990). *The perilous road.* Orlando, FL: Harcourt Brace.

Venezia, M. (1988). *Picasso.* Chicago: Children's Press.

Wisler, C. (1991). *Red cap.* New York: Lodestar Books.

Yenne, B. (1993). *100 events that shaped world history.* San Francisco: Bluewood Books.

References

Bamford, R., and Kristo, J. (Eds.). (1998). *Making facts come alive: Choosing quality nonfiction literature K-8.* Norwood, MA: Christopher-Gordon.

Bishop, R. S., & Hickman, J. (1992) "Four or fourteen or forty: Picture books are for everyone," in *Beyond words picture books for older readers and writers.* Portsmouth, NH: Heinemann.

Burke-Hengen, M. (1995). Telling points: Teaching social studies with literature. In *Building community: Social studies in the middle years.* ed. M. Burke-Hengen & T. Gillespie. Portsmouth, NH: Heinemann.

Cerullo, M. (1997). *Reading the environment: Children's literature in the science classroom.* Portsmouth, NH: Heinemann.

Daniels, H. (1994). *Literature Circles: voice and choice and in the student-centered classroom.* York, ME: Stenhouse.

El-Hindi (May 1998). Beyond classroom boundaries: Constructivist teaching with the Internet. *The Reading Teacher, 51,* 8, 694–700.

Kiefer, B. (1998). Creating possibilities, deepening appreciation: Nonfiction literature to study the arts. In *Making facts come alive: Choosing quality nonfiction literature K-8.* ed. R. A. Bamford & J. V. Kristo. Norwood, MA: Christopher-Gordon Pubs.

Palmer, R. G., & Stewart, R. A. (May 1997). Nonfiction trade books in content area instruction: Realities and potential. *Journal of Adolescent and Adult Literacy, 40* (8), 630–641.

Siu-Runyan, Y. (1995). Using literature to inquire and learn. In *Beyond separate subjects: Integrative learning at the middle Level* (pp. 131–156). ed. Y. Siu-Runyan, & C. V. Faircloth. Norwood, MA: Christopher-Gordon.

Stephens, E., & Brown, J. (1998).*Learning about . . . the civil war: Literature and other resources for young people.* North Haven, CT: Linnet Professional Publication.

Whitin, A. J., & Wilde, S. (1992). *Read any good math lately? Children's books for mathematical learning, K-6.* Norwood, MA: Christopher-Gordon.

Wilde, Sandra. (1998). Mathematical learning and exploration in nonfiction literature. In *Making facts come alive: Choosing quality nonfiction literature K-8.* ed. R. A. Bamford & J. V. Kristo. Norwood, MA: Christopher-Gordon.

Wilhelm, J. (1998). Big stuff at the middle level: the real world, real reading, and right action. In *Making facts come alive: Choosing quality nonfiction literature K-8.* ed. R. A. Bamford & J. V. Kristo. Norwood, MA: Christopher-Gordon.

APPENDIX A
Professional Organizations and Journals

International Reading Association (IRA)
800 Barksdale Rd., PO Box 8139
Newark, DE 19714-8139
Phone: (302) 731-1600
Fax: 302-731-1057
Internet: http://www.reading.org

National Council of Teachers of English (NCTE)
1111 W. Kenyon Road
Urbana, IL 61801-1096
Phone: (800) 369-6283
Fax: (217) 328-9645
Internet: http://www.ncte.org

National Council for the Social Studies (NCSS)
3501 Newark St. NW
Washington, D.C. 20016
Phone: 202-966-7840
Internet: http://www.ncss.org

National Council of Teachers of Mathematics
(NCTM)
1906 Association Drive
Reston, VA 20191-1593
Phone: (703) 620-9840
Fax: (703) 476-2970
E-Mail: nctm@nctm.org
Internet: http://www.nctm.org

National Science Teachers Association (NSTA)
1840 Wilson Blvd.
Arlington, VA 22201-3000
Phone: (703) 243-7100
Fax: (703) 243-7177
E-Mail: s&c@nsta.org
Internet: http://www.nsta.org

Book Links: Connecting Books, Libraries, and Classrooms
Bimonthly magazine from the American
Library Association
50 E. Huron St.
Chicago, IL
Phone for subscriptions: (603) 892-7465
Fax: (312) 337-6787
E-Mail: jomalley@ala.org
Internet: http://www.ala.org/BookLinks

The Bulletin of the Center for Children's Books
Monthly bulletin published by the Graduate
School of Library and Information Science of
the University of Illinois and the University of
Illinois Press
54 E. Gregory Drive
Champaign, IL 61820
Phone: (217) 333-8935

The Horn Book Magazine
Bimonthly publication of reviews and related
articles
14 Beacon Street
Boston, MA 02108-9765
Phone: (800) 325-1170

The New Advocate
Quarterly publication focusing on the connec-
tions between literature and teaching
1502 Providence Highway, Suite 12
Norwood, MA 02062
Phone: (781) 762-5577

School Library Journal
Monthly publication reviews new books and
publishes related articles
PO Box 1978
Marion, OH 43306-2078
Phone: (800) 842-1669

VOYA (Voice of Youth Advocates)
Bimonthly publication related to young adult
literature
Scarecrow Press
Dept. VOYA
52 Library Street
PO Box 4167
Metuchen, NJ 08840
Phone: (800) 537-7107

The WEB: Wonderfully Exciting Books
Published three times a year by the Center for
Language, Literature and Reading of the Ohio
State University; has reviews and ideas for
integrating literature into the school curriculum

APPENDIX B
Award-Winning Books

Jane Addams Book Award

The Jane Addams Children's Book Award has been presented annually since 1953 by the Women's International League for Peace and Freedom and the Jane Addams Peace Association to the children's book of the preceding year that most effectively promotes the cause of peace, social justice, and world community.

1998	Longer Book:	*Habibi* by Naomi Shihab Nye
	Picture Book:	*Seven Brave Women* by Betsy Hearne, illustrated by Bethanne Anderson
1997	Longer Book:	*Growing up in coal country* by Susan Campbell Bartoletti
	Picture Book:	*Wilma Unlimited* by Kathleen Krull, illustrated by David Diaz
1996	Longer Book:	*The Well* by Mildred D. Taylor
	Picture Book:	No award given.
	Special Commendation:	*The Middle Passage* by Tom Feelings
1995	Longer Book:	*Kids at Work: Lewis Hine and the Crusade Against Child Labor* by Russell Freedman
	Picture Book:	*Sitti's Secrets* by Naomi Shihab Nye, illustrated by Nancy Carpenter
1994	Longer Book:	*Freedom's Children: Young Civil Rights Activists Tell Their Stories* by Ellen Levine
	Picture Book:	*This Land Is My Land* by George Littlechild
1993	Longer Book:	*A Taste of Salt: A Story of Modern Haiti* by Frances Temple
	Picture Book:	*Aunt Harriet's Underground Railroad in the Sky* by Faith Ringgold

Americas Award

In 1993, the national Consortium of Latin American Studies Programs (CLASP) initiated a yearly children's and young adults book award, with a commended list of titles. Beginning in 1995, a new category of "Honorable Mentions" was added to properly recognize those books that contended as finalists for the award.

The award is given in recognition of a U.S. work (picture books, poetry, fiction, folklore) published in the previous year in English or Spanish which authentically and engagingly presents the experience of individuals in Latin America or the Caribbean, or of Latinos in the United States. By combining both and linking the Americas, the award reaches beyond geographic borders, as well as multicultural-international boundaries, focusing instead upon cultural heritages within the hemisphere. The award and the other commended books were selected for their quality of story, cultural authenticity/sensitivity, and potential for classroom use.

1997	Fiction:	*The Circuit: Stories from the life of a Migrant Child* by Francisco Jiménez
	Picture Book:	*The Face at the Window* by Regina Hanson, illustrated by Linda Saport
	Honorable Mention:	
		Fruits: A Caribbean Counting Poem by Valerie Bloom; illustrated by David Axtell
		Mayeros: A Yucatec Maya Family by George Ancona

1996   Picture Book: *In My Family/En Mi Familia* by Carmen Lomas Garza

        Fiction: *Parrot in the Oven: Mi Vida* by Victor Martínez

        Honorable Mention:

                Down by the River: Afro-Caribbean Rhymes, Games and Songs for Children, compiled by Grace Hallworth, illustrated by Caroline Binch

                So Loud a Silence by Lyll Becerra de Jenkins

1995   *Tonight by Sea* by Frances Temple

        Honorable Mention:

                An Island Like You: Stories of the Barrio by Judith Ortiz Cofer

                Chato's Kitchen by Gary Soto, illustrated by Susan Guevara

                Heart of a Jaguar by Marc Talbert

1994   *The Mermaid's Twin Sister: More Stories from Trinidad* by Lynn Joseph

Hans Christian Andersen Medals

Hans Christian Andersen Medals are awarded every two years to one author and one illustrator in recognition of his or her entire body of work by the International Board on Books for Young People.

1996   Author: Uri Orlev (Israel)
        Illustrator: Klaus Ensikat (Germany)

1994   Author: Michio Mado (Japan)
        Illustrator: Jörg Müller (Switzerland)

1992   Author: Virginia Hamilton (United States)
        Illustrator: Kveta Pacovska (Czechoslovakia)

1990   Author: Tormod Haugen (Norway)
        Illustrator: Lisbeth Zwerger (Austria)

The Mildred L. Batchelder Award

This award honors Mildred L. Batchelder, a former executive director of the Association for Library Service to Children and a staunch believer in the importance of good books for children in translation from all parts of the world. It is awarded annually to an American publisher for a children's book considered to be the most outstanding of those books originally published in a foreign language in a foreign country, and subsequently translated into English and published in the United States.

1999   Winner: *Thanks to My Mother* by Schoschana Rabinovici, 1998. Translated from the German by James Skofield.

1998   Winner: Henry Holt, for *The Robber and Me* by Josef Holub, edited by Mark Aronson and translated from the German by Elizabeth D. Crawford

        Honors: Scholastic, for *Hostage to War: A True Story* by Tatjana Wassiljewa, translated from German by Anna Trenter

                    Viking, for *Nero Corleone: A Cat's Story* by Elke Heidenrich, translated from German by Doris Orgel

1997   Winner: Farrar Straus Giroux, for *The Friends* by Kazumi Yumoto, translated from Japanese by Cathy Hirano

1996   Winner: Houghton Mifflin, for *The Lady with the Hat* by Uri Orlev, translated from Hebrew by Hillel Halikin

Honors: Holt, for *Damned Strong Love: The True Story of Willi G. and Stephan K.* by Lutz Van Dijk, translated from German by Elizabeth D. Crawford

Walker, for *Star of Fear, Star of Hope* by Jo Hoestlandt, translated from French by Mark Polizzotti

1995   Winner: Dutton, for *The Boys from St. Petri* by Bjarne Reuter, translated from Danish by Anthea Bell

Honor: Lothrop, for *Sister Shako and Kolo the Goat: Memories of My Childhood in Turkey* by Vedat Dalokay, translated from Turkish by Güner Ener

1994   Winner: Farrar, for *The Apprentice* by Pilar Molina Llorente, translated from Spanish by Robin Longshaw

Honors: Farrar, for *The Princess in the Kitchen Garden* by Annemie & Margriet Heymans, translated from Dutch by Johanna H. Prins and Johanna W. Prins

Viking, for *Anne Frank Beyond the Diary: A Photographic Remembrance* by Ruud van der Rol & Rian Verhoeven, in association with the Anne Frank House, translated from Dutch by Tony Langham and Plym Peters.

Boston Globe–Horn Book Award

This award has been presented annually since 1967 by the *Boston Globe* and the Horn Book magazine.

1998   Fiction: *The Circuit: Stories from the Life of a Migrant Child* by Francisco Jiminez
        Honors: *While No One Was Watching* by Jane Leslie Conly
                   My Louisiana Sky by Kimberly Willis Holt
        Nonfiction: *Leon's Story* by Leon Walter Tillage
        Honors: *Martha Graham: A Dancer's Life* by Russell Freedman
                   Chuck Close Up Close by Jan Greenberg
        Picture Book: *And if the Moon Could Talk* by Kate Banks, illustrated by Georg Hallensleben
        Honors: *Seven Brave Women* by Betsy Hearne, illustrated by Bethanne Anderson
                   Popcorn Poems written and illustrated by James Stevenson

1997   Fiction and Poetry: *The Friends* by Kazumi Yumoto, translated by Cathy Hirano
        Honors: *Lily's Crossing* by Patricia Reilly Giff
                   Harlem, written by Walter Dean Myers, illustrated by Christopher Myers
        Nonfiction: *A Drop of Water: A Book of Science and Wonder* by Walter Wick
        Honors: *Lou Gehrig: The Luckiest Man* by David A. Adler, illustrated by Terry Widener
                   Leonardo da Vinci by Diane Stanley
        Picture Book: *The Adventures of Sparrowboy* by Brian Pinkney
        Honors: *Home on the Bayou: A Cowboy's Story* by G. Brian Karas
                   Potato: A Tale from the Great Depression by Kate Lied, illustrated by Lisa Campbell Ernst

1996   Fiction: *Poppy* by Avi, illustrated by Brian Floca

	Honors:	*The Moorchild* by Eloise McGraw
		Belle Prater's Boy by Ruth White
	Nonfiction:	*Orphan Train Rider: One Boy's True Story* by Andrea Warren
	Honors:	*The Boy Who Lived with the Bears: And Other Iroquois Stories* by Joseph Bruchac, ill. by Murv Jacob
		Haystack by Bonnie and Arthur Geisert, illustrated by Arthur Geisert
	Picture Book:	*In the Rain with Baby Duck* by Amy Hest, illustrated by Jill Barton
	Honors:	*Fanny's Dream* by Caralyn Buehner, illustrated by Mark Buehner
		Home Lovely by Lynne Rae Perkins
1995	Fiction:	*Some of the Kinder Planets* by Tim Wynne-Jones
	Honors:	*Jericho* by Janet Hickman
		Earthshine by Theresa Nelson
	Nonfiction:	*Abigail Adams: Witness to a Revolution* by Natalie S. Bober
	Honors:	*It's Perfectly Normal: Changing Bodies, Growing Up, Sex, and Sexual Health* by Robie H. Harris, illustrated by Michael Emberley
		The Great Fire by Jim Murphy
	Picture Book:	*John Henry*, retold by Julius Lester, illustrated by Jerry Pinkney
	Honor:	*Swamp Angel* by Anne Isaacs, illustrated by Paul O. Zelinsky
1994	Fiction:	*Scooter* by Vera Williams
	Honors:	*Flour Babies* by Anne Fine)
		Western Wind by Paula Fox
	Nonfiction:	*Eleanor Roosevelt: A Life of Discovery* by Russell Freedman
	Honors:	*Unconditional Surrender: U.S. Grant and the Civil War* by Albert Marrin
		A Tree Place and Other Poems by Constance Levy, illustrated by Robert Sabuda
	Picture Book:	*Grandfather's Journey* by Allen Say
	Honors:	*Owen* by Kevin Henkes
		A Small Tall Tale from the Far Far North by Peter Sis
1993	Fiction:	*Ajeemah and His Son* by James Berry
	Honor:	*The Giver* by Lois Lowry
	Nonfiction:	*Sojourner Truth: Ain't I a Woman?* by Patricia C. and Fredrick McKissack
	Honor:	*Lives of the Musicians: Good Times, Bad Times (And What the Neighbors Thought)*, written by Kathleen Krull, illustrated by Kathryn Hewitt
	Picture Book:	*The Fortune Tellers* by Lloyd Alexander, illustrated by Trina Schart Hyman
	Honors:	*Komodo!* by Peter Sis
		Raven: A Trickster Tale from the Pacific Northwest by Gerald McDermott

The Margaret A. Edwards Award

The Margaret A. Edwards Award honors an author's lifetime achievement for writing books that have been popular with teenagers over a period of time.

1998	Madeleine L'Engle
1997	Gary Paulsen
1996	Judy Blume
1995	Cynthia Voight
1994	Walter Dean Meyers
1993	M. E. Kerr
1992	Lois Duncan
1991	Robert Cormier
1990	Richard Peck

IRA Children's Book Award

Presented annually by the International Reading Association to recognize informational books and outstanding fiction for younger and older readers.

1997–98	Younger	*Nim and the War Effort* by Milly Lee and Yangsook Choi
	Older	*Moving Mama to Town* by Ronder Thomas Young
	Informational	*Just What the Doctor Ordered: The History of American Medicine* by Brandon Marie Miller
1996–97	Younger	*More Than Anything Else* by Marie Bradby, illustrated by Chris K. Soentpiet
	Older	*The King's Shadow* by Elizabeth Alder
	Informational	*The Case of the Mummified Pigs and Other Mysteries in Nature* by Susan E. Quilan
1994–95	Younger	*The Ledgerbook of Thomas Blue Eagle* by Gay Mattaei and Jewel Grutman, illustrated by Adam Cvijanovis
	Older	*Spite Fences* by Trudy Krisher
	Informational	*Stranded at Plimoth Plantation 1626* by Gary Bowen
1993–94	Younger	*Sweet Clara and the Freedom Quilt* by Deborah Hopkinson
	Older	*Behind the Secret Window, A Memoir of a Secret Childhood During World War Two* by Nelly S. Toll

The Coretta Scott King Award

The Coretta Scott King Award honors African American authors and illustrators for outstanding contributions to children's and young adult literature that promote understanding and appreciation of the culture and contribution of all people to the realization of the American Dream. (Award Winners and Honor Books)

1999	Author Award Winner:	*Heaven* by Angela Johnson
	Honor Books:	*Jazmin's Notebook* by Nikki Grimes
		Breaking Ground, Breaking Silence: The Story of New York's African Burail Ground by Joyce Hansen and Gary McGowan
		The Other Side: Shorter Poems by Angela Johnson
	Illustrator Award Winner:	*I See the Rhythm,* illustrated by Michele Wood; text by Toyomi Igus.

Honor Books: *I Have Heard of a Land,* illustrated by Floyd Cooper; text by Joyce Carol Thomas

The Bat Boy and His Violin, illustrated by E.B. Lewis; text by Gavin Curtis

Duke Ellington: The Piano Prince and His Orchestra, illustrated by Brian Pinkney; text by Andrea Davis Pinkney

1998   Author Award Winner: *Forged by Fire* by Sharon M. Draper

Honor Books: *Bayard Rustin: Behind the Scenes of the Civil Rights Movement* by James Haskins

I Thought My Soul Would Rise and Fly: The Diary of Patsy, a Freed Girl by Joyce Hansen

Illustrator Award Winner: *In Daddy's Arms I am Tall: African Americans Celebrating Fathers,* illustrated by Javaka Steptoe; text by Alan Schroeder

Honor Books: *Ashley Bryan's ABC of African American Poetry* by Ashley Bryan

Harlem, illustrated by Christopher Myers; text by Walter Dean Myers

The Hunterman and the Crocodile by Baba Wagué Diakité

1997   Author Award Winner: *Slam* by Walter Dean Myers

Honor Book: *Rebels Against Slavery: American Slave Revolts* by Patricia C. & Frederick L. McKissack

Illustrator Award Winner: *Minty: A Story of Young Harriet Tubman,* illustrated by Jerry Pinkney; text by Alan Schroeder

Honor Books: *The Palm of My Heart: Poetry by African American Children,* illustrated by Gregorie Christie; ed. by David Adedjouma

Running the Road to ABC, illustrated by Reynold Ruffins; text by Denize Lauture

Neeny Coming, Neeny Going, illustrated by Synthia Saint James; text by Karen English

1996   Author Award Winner: *Her Stories* by Virginia Hamilton

Honor Books: *The Watsons Go to Birmingham—1963* by Christopher Paul Curtis

Like Sisters on the Homefront by Rita Williams-Garcia

From the Notebooks of Melanin Sun by Jacqueline Woodson

Illustrator Award Winner: *The Middle Passage: White Ships Black Cargo* by Tom Feelings

Honor Books: *Her Stories,* illustrated by Leo and Diane Dillon; text by Virginia Hamilton

The Faithful Friend, illustrated by Brian Pinkney; text by Robert San Souci

1995   Author Award Winner: *Christmas in the Big House, Christmas in the Quarters* by Patricia C. & Frederick L. McKissack

Honor Books: *The Captive* by Joyce Hansen

I Hadn't Meant to Tell You This by Jacqueline Woodson

Black Diamond: Story of the Negro Baseball League by Patricia C. & Frederick L. McKissack

Illustrator Award Winner: *The Creation,* illustrated by James Ransome; text by James Weldon Johnson

Honor Books: *The Singing Man,* illustrated by Terea Shaffer; text by Angela Shelf Medearis

Meet Danitra Brown, illustrated by Floyd Cooper; text by Nikki Grimes

1994   Author Award Winner: *Toning the Sweep* by Angela Johnson

        Honor Books: *Brown Honey in Broom Wheat Tea* by Joyce Carol Thomas; illustrated by Floyd Cooper

                                                            Malcolm X: By Any Means Necessary by Walter Dean Myers

    Illustrator Award Winner: *Soul Looks Back in Wonder*, illustrated by Tom Feelings; text ed. by Phyllis Fogelman

        Honor Books: Brown Honey in Broom Wheat Tea, illustrated by Floyd Cooper; text by Joyce Carol Thomas

                                                            Uncle Jed's Barbershop, illustrated by James Ransome; text by Margaree King Mitchell

Newbery Award

The Newbery Award, established in honor of the English publisher and bookseller, is presented annually by the American Library Association to the author of the most distinguished contribution to American literature for children published in the preceding year.

1999   Winner: *Holes* by Louis Sachar

        Honor Books: *A Long Way from Chicago* by Richard Peck

1998   Winner: *Out of the Dust* by Karen Hesse

        Honor Books: *Ella Enchanted* by Gail Carson Levine
                         Lily's Crossing by Patricia Reilly Giff
                         Wringer by Jerry Spinelli

1997   Winner: *The View from Saturday* by E. L. Konigsburg

        Honor Books: *A Girl Named Disaster* by Nancy Farmer
                         The Moonchild by Eloise Jarvis McGraw
                         The Thief by Megan Whalen Turner
                         Belle Prater's Boy by Ruth White

1996   Winner: *The Midwife's Apprentice* by Karen Cushman

        Honor Books: *What Jamie Saw* by Carolyn Coman
                         The Watsons Go to Birmingham—1963 by Christopher Paul Curtis
                         Yolonda's Genius by Carol Fenner
                         The Great Fire by Jim Murphy

1995   Winner: *Walk Two Moons* by Sharon Creech

        Honor Books: *Catherine, Called Birdy* by Karen Cushman
                         The Ear, the Eye, and the Arm by Nancy Farmer

1994   Winner: *The Giver* by Lois Lowry

        Honor Books: *Crazy Lady!* by Jane Leslie Conly
                         Dragon's Gate by Laurence Yep
                         Eleanor Roosevelt: A Life of Discovery by Russell Freedman

Scott O'Dell Award for Historical Fiction

Established in 1981 by Scott O'Dell and administered by the Bulletin of the Center for Children's Book, this award recognizes historical fiction of literary merit set in the new world.

1998   *Out of the Dust* by Karen Hesse
1997   *Jib: His Story* by Katherine Paterson
1996   *The Bomb* by Theodore Taylor

1995   *Under the Blood Red Sun* by Graham Salisbury
1994   *Bull Run* by Paul Fleischman

Orbis Pictus

Presented annually by the National Council of Teachers of English to honor distinction in nonfiction for children.

1998	Winner:	*An Extraordinary Life: The Story of a Monarch Butterfly* by Laurence Pringle, illustrated by Bob Marstall
	Honor Book:	*A Drop of Water: A Book of Science and Wonder* by Walter Wick
		A Tree is Growing by Arthur Dorros, illustrated by S. D. Schindler
		Charles A. Lindbergh: A Human Hero by James Cross Giblin
		Kennedy Assassinated! The World Mourns: A Reporter's Story by Wilborn Hampton
		Digger: The Tragic Fate of the California Indians from the Missions to the Gold Rush by Jerry Stanley
1997	Winner:	*Leonardo da Vinci* by Diane Stanley
	Honor Books	*Full Steam Ahead: The Race to Build a Transcontinental Railroad* by Rhoda Blumberg
		The Life and Death of Crazy Horse by Russell Freedman
		One World, Many Religions: The Way We Worship by Mary Pope Osborne
1996	Winner:	*The Great Fire* by Jim Murphy
	Honor Books:	*Dolphin Man: Exploring the World of Dolphins* by Laurence Pringle
		Rosie the Riveter: Women Working on the Home Front in World War II by Penny Colman
1995	Winner:	*Safari Beneath the Sea: The Wonder of the North Pacific Coast* by Diane Swanson
	Honor Books:	*Wildlife Rescue: The Work of Dr. Kathleen Ramsay* by Jennifer Owings Dewy
		Kids at Work: Lewis Hine and the Crusade Against Child Labor by Russell Freedman
		Christmas in the Big House, Christmas in the Quarters by Patricia McKissack and Frederick McKissack
1994	Winner:	*Across America on an Emigrant Train* by Jim Murphy
	Honor Books:	*To the Top of the World: Adventures with Arctic Wolves* by Jim Brandenburg
		Making Sense: Animal Perception and Communication by Bruce Brooks

Phoenix Award

The Phoenix Award was established 1985 by the Children's Literature Association. It is awarded annually to a book originally published in English twenty years previously which did not receive a major award at the time of its publication.

2000	Winner:	Monica Hughes, *The Keeper of the Isis Light*
1999	Winner:	E. L. Konigsburg, *Throwing Shadows*
1998	Winner:	Jill Paton Walsh, *A Chance Child*
	Honor Books:	Robin McKinley, *Beauty*
		Doris Orgel, *The Devil in Vienna*

1997	Winner:	Robert Cormier, *I Am the Cheese*
1996	Winner:	Alan Garner, *The Stone Book*
	Honor Book:	William Steig, *Abel's Island*
1995	Winner:	Laurence Yep, *Dragonwings*
	Honor Book:	Natalie Babbitt, *Tuck Everlasting*
1994	Winner:	Katherine Paterson, *Of Nightingales that Weep*
	Honor Books:	James Lincoln Collier and Christopher Collier, *My Brother Sam is Dead*
		Sharon Bell Mathis, *Listen for the Fig Tree*

The Laura Ingalls Wilder Medal

Administered by the Association for Library Service to Children, a division of the American Library Association, the Laura Ingalls Wilder Award was first given to its namesake in 1954. The award, a bronze medal, honors an author or illustrator whose books, published in the United States, have made, over a period of years, a substantial and lasting contribution to literature for children. Between 1960 and 1980, the Wilder Award was given every five years. Since 1983, it has been awarded every three years.

Recipients:

1998	Russell Freedman
1995	Virginia Hamilton
1992	Marcia Brown
1989	Elizabeth George Speare
1986	Jean Fritz
1983	Maurice Sendak
1980	Theodor S. Geisel (Dr. Seuss)
1975	Beverly Cleary
1970	E. B. White
1965	Ruth Sawyer
1960	Clara Ingram Judson
1954	Laura Ingalls Wilder

Carter G. Woodson Award

Presented annually since 1973 by the National Council for the Social Studies, the award recognizes trade books that provide a "multicultural or multiethnic perspective." (E is for elementary level; S for secondary.)

1997	*Leon's Story* by Leon Walter Tillage (E)
	Langston Hughes, an illustrated edition by Milton Meltzer (S)
1996	*Songs from the Loom: A Navajo Girl Learns to Weave* by Monte Roessel (E)
	A Fence Away from Freedom by Ellen Levine (S)
1995	*What I Had Was Singing: The Story of Marian Anderson* by Jeri Ferris (E)
	Till Victory Is Won: Black Soldiers in the Civil War by Zak Mettger (S)
1994	*Starting Home: The Story of Horace Pippin, Painter* by Mary E. Lyon (E)
	The March on Washington by Jim Haskins (S)

APPENDIX C
Listservs and Web Sites

Listservs

The following listservs are representative of those available for teachers and, in some cases, students to have the opportunity to share ideas in a focused area.

NCTE-talk—send message to	listproc@itc.org
	Subscribe NCTE-talk
English teacher list—send message to	majordomo@ux1.cso.uiuc.edu
	subscribe English-teachers
BR_Cafe kids talk books—send message to	listproc@micronet.wcu.edu
	SUBSCRIBE BR_Cafe and name
BR_Review k–12 book reviews—send message to	listproc@micronet.wcu.edu
	SUBSCRIBE BR_Review and name
STORYTELL-REQUEST@VENUS.TWU.EDU	subscribe
listproc@schoolnet.carleton.ca	subscribe childrens-voice
HarperCollins	lists@info.harpercollins.com
	subscribe childrenslibrary
Issues for reading professionals:	majordomo@indiana.edu
	subscribe readpro
listserv@bingvmb.cc.binghamton.edu	subscribe KIDLIT-L
listserv@rutvm1.rutgers.edu	subscribe CHILDLIT
Readers Theatre	Subscribe RTEACHER@LISTSERV.SYR.EDU

Selected Book Review, Indices, and Database Sources

Please note that the URLs for web sites change frequently.

Book Nook	http://I-site.on.ca/booknook.html
Children's Literature	http://www.parentsplace.com/readroom/childnew/index/html
Connections Children's Book News	http://community.net/~benchun/bookafair/21.html
Database of Award Winning Children's Literature	http://www2.wcoil.com/~ellerbee/childlit.html
Doucette Index-K-12 Teaching Ideas for Literature	http://www.educ.ucalgary.ca/litindex/
Horn Book Guide	http://www.hbook.com/guide.html
Midwest Book Review Children's Book Watch	http://www.execpc.com/%7Embr/bookwatch/cbw/#rc
Notes from the Windowsill Book Reviews	http://www.armory.com/~web/notes.html
The ALAN Review	http://www.scholar.lib.vt.edu/ejournals?ALAN/alan-review.html
Young Adult Reading	http://www.docker.com/~whiteheadm/yaread.html

Selected Sites for Young Adult and Children's Literature

ALA	http://www.ala.org/alsc/
Center for the Study of Young Adult Literature	http://www.concentric.net/~jebrown/

Children's Book Council	http://www.cbcbooks.org/
Children's Fiction	http://www.primenet.com/~callie/children.htm
Children's Literature Guide	http://www.unm.edu/~lhendr
The Children's Literature Web Guide	http://www.ucalgary.ca/~dkbrown/listserv.html
ENC Focus—Using Literature in Math and Science	http://enc.org/classroom/focus/childlit
ERIC	http://www.indiana.edu/~eric_rec/ieo/bibs/adol-lit.html
Internet Public Library	http://ipl.sils.umich.edu/youth/
	http://www.ipl.org/teen/
Kids Web Literature	http://www.npac.syr.edu/textbook/kidsweb/literature/html
Montage—Mary Ellen Van Camp's Web Page on Children's and Young Adult Literature	http://nova.bsuvc.bsc.edu/~..mevancamp/montage.html
National Council for the Social Studies Notable Children's Books	http://www.ncss.org/online/publications/booklist.html
Newbery Medal Home Page	http://www. ala.org/alsc/newbery.html
Readers Theatre	http://www.stemnet.nf.ca/CITE/langrt.htm#Gander
Reading List	http://www.echonyc.com/~cafephrk/angstbooks.html
Reading Rants: Teen Booklists	http://tln.lib.mi.us/~amutch/jen/index.html
Scholastic Magazine	http://scholastic.com:2005/
Storyreading Home Page	http://www.wco.com/~gailg/storyreading/
Vandergrift's Children's Literature Page	http://www.scils.rutgers.edu/special/kay/childlit.html
Vandergrift's Young Adult Literature Page	http://www.scils.rutgers.edu/special/kay/yalit.html
Young Adult Literature	http://www.ct.net/~patem/yalit/
Young Adult Literature	http://freenet.vcu.edu/education/literature/yalit.html

Author Pages

This list is selective to represent different ways that author pages are created, for example, by the authors themselves, by publisher, by organizations, or by readers.

Internet Public Library	http://www. ipl.org/youth/AskAuthor/
Author Corner	http:www.carr.lib.md.us/authco/home.htm
Avon Books	http://www.avonbooks.com
Bantam Doubleday Dell	www.bdd.com/index.html
Avi	http://www.avi-writer.com/
Joan Bauer	http://www.joanbauer.com
Chris Crutcher	http://www. www.bdd.bin/forums/teachers/crut.html
Christopher Paul Curtis	http://www.indiana.edu/-eric-recieo/bibs/curtis.html
Karen Cushman	http://www. eduplace.com/rdg/author/cushman/index.html
Lois Duncan	http://www.iag,net/-barq/lois.htmI
Virginia Hamilton	http://www.members.aol.com/bodeep/index.htmi
Brian Jacques	http://www.www.redwall.org
Madeleine L'Engle	http://www. geocities.com.Athens/Acropolis/8838/
Mary E. Lyons	http://www.comet.net/writerssc/lyonsden/index.htm
Katherine Paterson	http://www.terabithia.com/
Gary Paulsen	http//www.bdd.com/bin/forums/teachers/paul.html
Paul Pullman	http://www.randomhouse.com/goidencompass/
Carolyn Reeder	http://www.childrensbookguideorg/Reeder.html

INDEX

A

About the Authors

Elaine C. Stephens

Jean E. Brown

Elaine C. Stephens and Jean E. Brown are both Professors of Teacher Education at Saginaw Valley State University, Michigan where they teach courses in reading, writing, and literature. Collectively, they have had more than 50 years of teaching experience in public schools, colleges, and universities. *A Handbook of Content Literacy Strategies* is the 10th book they have written together. Their other books include:

> *Toward Literacy: Theory and Practice in Teaching Writing in the Content Areas* (with Lela Phillips)
>
> *Young Adult Literature in the Classroom: Sharing the Connections*
>
> *Exploring Diversity: Literature, Themes, and Activities*
>
> *Learning about the Holocuast...Literature and Other Resources for Young People* (with Janet Rubin)
>
> *Images from the Holocaust* (with Janet Rubin)
>
> *United in Diversity: Using Multicultural Young Adult Literature*
>
> *Learning About...the Civil War: Literature and Other Resources for Young People*
>
> *Two Way Street: Integrating Reading and Writing in the Middle Schools* (with Barbara Quirk);
>
> *Two Way Street: Integrating Reading and Writing in the Secondary Schools* (with Barbara Quirk);

Stephens and Brown are active in professional organizations and are co-editors of the Book Review column for the *SIGNAL Journal* and the Research Connection for the *ALAN Review*. They have received numerous awards for teaching, research, and service, including recognition from the Michigan Association of Governing Boards of State Universities for "distinguished teaching and extraordinary contributions to higher education."